FULL
Immersion

FULL
Immersion

A Memoir about Caregiving,
Unconditional Love, and
Finding a Life of My Own

NANCY KOENIG

ILLUMIFY
IllumifyMedia.com

The views and opinions expressed in this book are those of the author and do not necessarily reflect the official policy or position of Illumify Media Global.
Published by Illumify Media Global
www.IllumifyMedia.com
"Write. Publish. Market. *SELL!*"

Library of Congress Control Number: 2019911992.
Paperback ISBN: 978-1-949021-51-6
eBook ISBN: 978-1-949021-56-1

Cover design by Debbie Lewis

Printed in the United States of America

To the women in my family now in heaven—my grandmother, Nellie, my mother, Lorraine, and my aunt, Helen—whose lives were not always as they planned but whose inspiration and influence in my life continue still. You were stronger than you knew. Can't wait to hear your voices once again.

CONTENTS

ACKNOWLEDGMENTS

I would like to express my special gratitude to my husband, Denny, for supporting my full immersion determination to tell my story. Thank you for being my cheering section. I love you.

I also want to acknowledge numerous colleagues who became friends:

Wendy, the best teammate I could have asked for, who became my best friend and confidante, the sister and daughter I never had. You are a special woman, always encouraging and loving, able to see the positive in everything. Thank you for being you.

Elizabeth, my kind, generous, patient friend, fellow lover of music, history, and the good in people and in our nation. Thank you for your unity of spirit as you partnered with me to support our Veteran's Day, Night of the Notables, and Literacy Nights programs. You are amazing.

Tina, my dear friend, though we came to know each other later, your unwavering support of me pursuing my dream propelled me forward when I questioned my decision (and sometimes my sanity). Here's to turning the page to see what the next chapter of life has for both of us. You don't have to figure it out all at once. Just focus on what can be done today.

I would like to thank the Illumify team, especially "Coach Karen," for making it possible for this story to be told. Thank you for sharing your knowledge and expertise with me.

Finally, a heartfelt thanks to all my wonderful students, families, and friends. Thank you for your full immersion influence in my life. Though teaching and learning can be tough, there are no more noble endeavors than these. It does not matter what's been written in your story so far. It's how you fill up the rest of the pages that counts.

INTRODUCTION

You have a unique, special story. Each of us does, yet while our experiences are ours alone, they are not unusual to humankind.

We all have similar needs—for example, the need to feel good enough, to be loved and secure, to achieve a sense of God-confidence, and to have a healthy sense of self.

In addition, we are each on a journey toward self-knowledge, and on this journey we often discover a sense of identity, purpose, and place even as we are filled with anticipation of the next stage.

Finally, we have in common many of life's events, although how we experience and respond to these events can feel radically unique. Moderation in all things is best, so we're told in Philippians 4:5, yet the challenges of this are substantial at times in our lives. Instead of moderation, we often resort to extreme response patterns and strategies, such as overworking, over- or under-eating, and depression, and these coping mechanisms often become our "normal." We find comfort in "but we've always done it like that" ways of being and thinking.

One of my purposes in sharing my story is to continue my own healing, to see through a new perspective only time can provide. In telling my story, I tell the stories of many of my students and their families. Many of the names have been changed to protect people's privacy. Much of my life has already been lived (six-plus decades), and I have observed that the past does not define my present but serves as a reminder to focus on accomplishing what God calls me to do with excellence, not perfection. Trying to please everyone drove me to be an achiever, but it also stifled my being truly happy for so long. I had been pushing on a door that said pull and asking God, "Is it okay to be happy? Is it okay to try something new? Is it okay to redirect all my intensity to other paths? Will I have a turn at living?" The answer was "yes" to each question, although "not yet" often seemed to be implied.

Another of my purposes in sharing my story is to be an encourager and a blessing—perhaps even a part of someone else's miracle. My experiences are unique to me, but their impact led me to make life-changing choices and to grow as a caregiver, daughter, sister, friend, teacher, wife—and most significantly as a child of God. My hope is that as you reflect with me about my life experiences, you will find encouragement for your own personal journey. Perhaps something I share in these pages will resonate for you and lead you to connect with what's truly significant for you. And my prayer is that, in the process, any default self-doubting statements that replay again and again in your thinking will find rest. Instead, that a new set of essential questions—"What matters most? What inspires you? What doors is God opening to the next step for you?"—will ultimately become your new default mind-set.

Regardless of what you may have been told (and perhaps even currently believe), you *are* good enough, you *do* have a purposeful story that God is revealing each day, and it really *is* okay to do what brings you joy.

And remember, perfection is not required.

Psalm 31:14–15 says, "But as for me, I trust in You, O Lord; I say, 'You are my God.' My times are in your hand" (NKJV). Furthermore, 1 Peter 5:10–11 tells us, "But the God of all grace, who hath called us unto his eternal glory by Christ Jesus, after that ye have suffered a while, make you perfect, stablish, strengthen, settle you. To him be glory and dominion for ever and ever. Amen." In the amazing understanding of who God is and what He is doing, we are secure, realizing that even our failures and our sins are under His control. We are indeed perfect and complete but only in Christ.

ONE

FULL IMMERSION

I suppose I have always been a "full immersion" person. I would define a full immersion person as someone who gives 100 percent to everything in life—including people, tasks, and goals—often multitasking to achieve an intended outcome. I have always done whatever needed to be done, which sometimes meant tackling endeavors I wasn't sure I could manage but found a way because it seemed necessary. What makes challenges more profound for me is that I feel deeply and care intensely about everything I do and everyone around me.

Dictionary definitions of *immersion* include synonyms such as absorption, concentration, engagement, diligence, attentiveness, captivation, and preoccupation. For me, full immersion also means intensity of focus and resiliency. I suppose this is both good news and bad news. After all, we all have a need for control, security, competency, and self-esteem. And while a full immersion mind-set has a lot of benefits, it can also become a self-protective strategy, a commitment to personal power with the goal of success or even perfection. It might even be considered a method of covering up the vulnerabilities and insecurities so many of us hide each day.

To be honest, I've come to believe that full immersion thinking is akin to "shadow boxing," a self-protective strategy to keep from being "found out," as in found out that I am not as smart or as good as my peers. In a world so intense with competition, being a fully immersed overachiever hedges one's bet that some level of acceptance will be achieved.

Perhaps you are a full immersion person too.

Those of us who are full immersion individuals can be viewed by others around us as "workhorses." We are the ones who will go the extra mile and contribute above and beyond expectations, hopefully crafting amazing outcomes in the process. We are the ones who are quite adept at delaying reward for our labor.

But what others don't always know is that full immersion folks are sometimes "human doings" aspiring to be human beings. We are not bold, outgoing, life-of-the-party "type A" folks, but kind, caring, quiet, self-sacrificing "type A" folks. We might even be peacemaker, figure-it-out-to-survive "type A" folks.

The point is that what drives us may not be immediately identifiable because we keep it hidden. Only our few select friends know that our motivation and drive to succeed are manifestations of our search for the missing pieces of ourselves. In total immersion of mind, heart, and soul in our work, we create a sense of control, reduce unpredictability, gain personal identity, and increase self-esteem and pride in our accomplishment. We finally have the evidence we long for that we are good enough.

This quality was not labeled for me until I was forty-three years old and essentially beginning life anew after three decades as a caregiver to my brother who became a quadriplegic after a diving accident at age twenty (I was twelve), as well as to my mother who suffered from Alzheimer's and dementia during the last three years of her life. Talk about being full immersion! Of course, I lived fully immersed in these heavy responsibilities out of need and responsibility, not by choice.

It has been my experience that when it's time to make big changes in life, God often reveals the path in amazing yet subtle ways. Sometimes His direction appears as a coincidental meeting or conversation. Sometimes it is an opportunity that you never considered before. Sometimes the new direction becomes clear when you are required to take on a challenge that only He can see you through. As God has provided people to lead me strategically when I needed them most, the saying "It is who you know, not what you know" has repeatedly proven true for me.

Life is all about timing and being open to change. This timing is not necessarily our own, though, and we are required to be open and to allow the old to make the new possible. A growth mind-set, as educators refer to it, is a "God mind-set."

In 1999 I found myself in Edmond, Oklahoma, serving as a caregiver for both my brother and my mother. It was a difficult time, and when I wasn't sure how I could possibly continue doing what I was required to do, God called my mom home to glory. I traveled with her body to Michigan so she could be laid to rest in Grand Rapids, her cherished hometown. While I was there, a dear family friend and a family member I had not seen in years were used of God to speak to me.

They told me it was finally time for me to have a life of my own.

They were right.

And so it began. In the year 2000, at age forty-three and after more than thirty years of caregiving in some form or another, I embarked on a new century and a new life—so much was changing. God's "yes" was becoming real. The "not yet" was becoming "now."

But I am getting ahead of myself . . .

Perhaps my penchant for resilience and overachievement cannot be blamed entirely on me. It seems I come from a long line of full immersion ancestors.

TWO

I WAS BORN TOO LATE

I always felt that, born in 1957, I arrived just a little too late. I was born too late for big bands, jukeboxes, poodle skirts, saddle shoes, and ice cream sundaes at the corner malt shop.

I was, however, born in time for movie musicals such as *My Fair Lady, The King and I, West Side Story, The Music Man,* and of course *The Sound of Music,* which I watched so many times I could have been a stand-in for Julie Andrews!

My mom and I went downtown—Grand Rapids, Michigan—on Saturday afternoons whenever possible to shop and go to the movies. We would shop in the old department stores—Steketee's, Herpolsheimer's, Wurzburg's—where personalized customer service was a priority and purchases were wrapped in tissue paper and boxed to carry home as if they were prizes.

Each building boasted a rich history of decades of welcoming guests, sheltering shoppers and downtown office workers from the rain and snow, and announcing every annual celebration with colorful banners and holiday displays. The unique charm of each storefront was carried through the interior with creaking wood plank floors, an aged musty smell, and lighting that was never bright but created a warm welcoming ambiance drawing guests in and encouraging them to stay. Shopping was an experience to remember, offering unique treasures of a quality not so commonly found in today's mass appeal marketing.

Time with my mom was always special. Born in 1925, she had a childhood compromised by the Great Depression and its aftermath, causing her to grow up to adult responsibilities too soon. Her relationship with her mother may have been impacted by a necessary focus on making ends meet, perhaps depriving her of needed intimacy. Later, once she became a mom herself, because of the nine-year age span between my brother and me, I could often do "girl stuff" with my mother almost as if I were an only child. Maybe in those hours I helped fill the need for the best friend or sister she never had (she had two older half brothers and a younger brother), in addition to my role as the daughter she waited nine years to have.

We would peek into Hoffman Jewelers with its elegant crystal chandeliers, ornate rounded wood molding, sparkling leaded-glass display cases, and fancy parlor-style carpet. We would go to the bank with its vault virtually impenetrable, with a door so heavy it required two people to close. The "ship's wheel" door handle spun to ensure its closure. The bank tellers were separated by glass, inaccessible to patrons unless invited to engage. I always found this space—which was open only nine to five, Monday through Friday, true banker's hours!—to be quiet and orderly, almost reverent.

When I needed new shoes, the place to go was VanHoecks or Mieras for Stride Rite. First, of course, the size of my foot was determined on the metal slide foot measurement tool, and boxes filled with the perfect style, color, and size of shoes were brought from the back of the store by a knowledgeable salesperson who would then expertly slip the shoes onto my feet. I vividly remember the magenta/burgundy orthopedic shoes I wore for years. (Oh, how I hated those shoes but am thankful today that Mom knew best.)

Probably every child takes the obligatory dance lessons. In my case I did not have the body type for ballet, so I took tap lessons. The dance studio was conveniently located directly above an ice cream shop called Jersey Junction, which was aptly named since Jersey is a British breed of small dairy cattle producing ten times their own weight in rich creamy milk each day. An ice cream shop below a dance studio is like a donut shop next to a health club. Mom would hand me money to buy an ice cream. I got a Blue Moon cone every time.

My mother was not an easy target for anything, especially for unearned rewards. She believed in working for what you wanted. The responsibility to manage money was valued and instilled in me at an early age. Saving was considered vital to ensure a future of choice, not want. And rewards were more special when planned for and anticipated. One such reward was a Saturday afternoon trip to F. W. Woolworth's five-and-ten store. Woolworth's was an intriguing mix of today's Walmart, Walgreens, and Ace Hardware. It truly had something for everyone.

In a child's eyes, the best of Woolworth's, besides the toy department, was the lunch counter. The grilled cheese sandwich with chips, pickle spear, and tomato soup (with oyster crackers, of course) were delicious, not to mention the banana split dessert! Talk about a reward! Absolutely amazing!

The idea of banana splits makes me smile to this day remembering how my mom would tell me about her mother and the joy they found in tough times by laughing together and sharing a banana split.

Being full immersion must be a dominant hereditary trait in the women of my family tree. I have never done an Ancestry.com search (although I probably should), but the women I am familiar with have stepped up, done what was necessary, and given God the praise for the outcomes.

Diligent, determined, responsible, perhaps a bit stubborn, Grandma Nellie was one of these women. Her first husband was institutionalized due to softening of the brain. She was not able to get a job, as married women were not considered employable. She had to divorce him in order to be able to support herself and her two sons. In 1914 she married my grandfather, who provided the home she needed for her and her two sons. My mother came along eleven years later in 1925. Grandma Nellie died when I was four, but I have a memory of a tall gray-haired lady who wore spectacles and had a kind heart and a snuggly lap made for sitting in and listening to stories. My mother credits the hours Grandma read aloud to me as the reason I learned to read at a very young age.

My grandparents were survivors of the Great Depression, having lost much of what they had worked so hard for. My grandfather lost his job and their car and later had to move his family because there was too little money to make a house payment. I was told that for a while he took Grandma's homemade donuts to sell in the nearby park, providing a treat for anyone with a nickel to spare.

He finally got a job with President Roosevelt's CCC (Civilian Conservation Corps) and helped build many of the parks that still exist all around Grand Rapids. Eventually Grandma landed work cleaning a dentist's office. She and my mom would go there in the evenings and on Saturdays and work as a team. Their reward for a completed week of work? A banana split.

My mother was also a survivor, a full immersion person even in her youth. She would ride the bus to her after-school job at Woolworth's. While attending high school, she learned typing, stenography, and transcription for future secretarial employment. She helped to support the family through the Depression years, learning how to make do with less, be creative, stretch what she had, and plan ahead for rationed items created during the war effort in the 1940s.

My mother married Edgar Walter Kent after he returned home from the navy, and my brother, David, was born in 1948. She worked full-time and cared for her child, her husband, her home, and later for me after I was born in 1957. Her mother died at home from a stroke at age seventy-three. Her father lived for several years in a nursing care facility before passing due to kidney failure at age eighty-four.

Then in 1969 my brother had a diving accident which permanently changed the lives of our entire family.

My mother's courageous determination to see him receive the best possible care and rehabilitation was immensely powerful! This strong commitment to doing right, taught to her by her parents and passed on to my brother and myself, was also a common characteristic in the culture of my hometown.

THREE

HOMETOWN

My southwestern Michigan hometown has a unique personality from a cultural mixture of English, German, and Dutch immigrants. The Christian Reformed church was well established and ever-present around the entire southwestern Michigan region. Names such as Vandenberg, Vander Wal, VanDerBeek, Oosterhaven, and Mueller were prominent. I remember registering for my first classes at Calvin College, a Dutch, Christian Reformed university, and being looked at strangely, as though an alien, when I stated my last name— Kent. Fortunately, they let me prove myself without judging me too harshly over my name!

Grand Rapids, the second largest city in Michigan, was founded in 1826. It is next to the Grand River and about thirty miles inland from Lake Michigan. Known for furniture production and its close proximity to forests and lakes, Grand Rapids is home to the Gerald R. Ford Presidential Library and Museum, the John Ball Zoo, the Pantlind Hotel which became the Amway Grand Plaza Hotel, and the Van Andel Arena.

The Thornapple River and Reeds Lake are astoundingly beautiful especially in the fall when the leaves change to yellows, oranges, and reds. The many apple orchards and pumpkin farms boast cider and doughnuts, other amazingly tempting treats, and hayrides. The fall snows bring skiing, snowshoeing, tobogganing, and the like. The holiday light displays are a must-see.

I vividly recall as a child enjoying the summer band concerts, the Fourth of July fireworks celebrations, our trips to Holland to walk in the sand, walks out on the pier to the lighthouse, the strong smell of fish, and the feel of the spray from the waves crashing up on the rocks. The most amazing adventures for me were ferry boat rides across Lake Huron to Mackinac Island's Fort Mackinac, with the Victorian-era Grand Hotel (built in 1887), and visits to the Henry Ford Museum in Dearborn outside of Detroit. Oh, the wonders these places had to offer! For my mother they perhaps fulfilled her need for some of the childhood experiences she did not have, and for me they created a sense of family that unfortunately would be short-lived.

Even though time and progress change our hometowns, and time and distance change each of us, our concepts of home never really change much. I have lived in several other cities and states, have grown in knowledge and understanding of the world, but still find a place in my heart that only memories of Grand Rapids will fill. This is where I grew up, where I journeyed from and back to. This is where my new life began at age forty-three and where my husband-to-be asked me to marry him when I was forty-five. This is the place where my birth family is buried. My chosen family is still a work in process. I am the only member of my birth family left. I am one of the newer members of my chosen family. This too is an example of full immersion at work: reaching out, planning, working toward goals, and finding self-esteem, personal worth, a sense of place, and self-acceptance.

Hometowns are unique, special places, profoundly important in the formation of our connections to our heritage, beliefs about ourselves, and understanding of the world around us. For better or worse, hometowns provide the foundations for the rest of our lives. Whether we long to be back in them or wish to be away from them, they are integrally a piece of who we are.

FOUR

AUGUST 23, 1969

My father was never a positive participant in my life.

By the time I was old enough to recognize my need for a positive dad role model, mental illness had overtaken his ability to interact rationally with the world. I remember him only once telling me that he loved me. He said the words through a locked bathroom door after my mother had served him with divorce papers. My impression even then, at age fourteen, was that I was his bargaining chip in a desperate bid to stop the unraveling of his marriage and life that had been going on for the past decade.

It didn't work.

My brother once shared that this man—who sat in the corner, eerily grinning due to some internal dialogue, smoking cigars, and sneaking around hiding things in the upstairs bedroom he had once shared with my mother—used to be the source of a fairly positive relationship for him. David knew he had gotten the best parenting years my dad had to offer before losing his battle to whatever schizophrenic thoughts so highly impacted him.

David also knew that he needed to be out on his own, away from what he saw happening. And so he worked very hard to finish his education, volunteering at the hospital emergency room in the evenings. As soon as he was able to leave for college, he headed to Kalamazoo College in Kalamazoo, Michigan. He took all the premed courses required to prepare him for medical school. And when the opportunity arose to travel abroad in the early spring of his junior year of college, he fled to Germany. David returned six months later with more hair on his face than he had on his balding head, and with a confidence not so evident in the past.

While I was stuck at home, navigating the treacherous waters around my father, it appeared that David had found the wings to fly.

Timing is everything, and God's timing often takes us by surprise. This was certainly true one hot Saturday afternoon in August 1969. I was twelve years old, and I had just sat down with my parents for supper at the picnic table on the patio in our backyard.

I loved our backyard. It was quiet and serene, private because of the six-foot-tall redwood fence that encompassed it. I had painted and stained this fence so many times I knew it up close and personal. The grass was lush and deep green as the summer sun and the ample rain had encouraged it to grow strong. On occasion we had lawn dart games and croquet matches, played frisbee, ran through the sprinkler, or simply lounged in the summer sun. I often studied there for hours while working on my summer tan. My mom's gorgeous rose-bushes climbed a trellis against the garage wall and on the side of the house up the chimney wall. She had a green thumb for rosebushes!

When the phone rang, my dad ran back into the house to answer. He called to my mom to come to the phone. Through the open window, I could hear their voices raise, and I knew something tragic had occurred.

The next moments were a frenzy of activity. The long-anticipated meal was abandoned as we hurried to the car and headed to Blodgett Hospital. It wasn't until we were waiting in the ER entrance that I learned what had happened.

David had been enjoying a pre-semester party at one of his professor's homes on a lake in Three Rivers, Michigan. He had been swimming all afternoon and decided to go for one more dip in the lake prior to calling it a day. Rather than shallow water dive as he had all afternoon, he dove too deeply, striking the bottom with enough force to snap his spinal cord in multiple places.

As a premed student, he immediately realized what he had done. Paralysis began to creep up his body, sensation and muscle control gone. One of David's friends pulled him to shore. Someone else called 911. When David insisted that he be taken back to Grand Rapids, the ambulance began the three-hour journey from Three Rivers to Grand Rapids.

In an attempt to prevent further nerve damage, the paramedic with David in the ambulance held his head still for the entire trip. This blessed young man was so stiff from being in this one position for so long that he had to be helped out of the ambulance when it finally arrived.

I will never forget the length of time we waited (it seemed an eternity), the angst my mother felt (that I could not help relieve), nor the paleness of my brother's face as his gurney was lifted from the ambulance and taken into the ER.

Our long wait continued.

When David's physician finally came out to the waiting room to speak to us, the prognosis was devastating. He anticipated that David would not live through the night.

I looked at my mother, my adolescent brain racing at full speed. *How can I make this better? How can I help my mom get through this? What's going to happen to David and how can I help him?*

To the astonishment of his physician, David did survive the night. He survived weeks in the hospital on a Stryker frame, burr holes on each side of his skull to attach the weights providing traction to aid in resetting the spinal column. Every few hours, medical staff rotated David from his back to his stomach—and vice versa—to prevent pressure sores from forming.

Those weeks in the hospital were followed by months of rehabilitation to stabilize, strengthen, and retrain the remaining functional body systems to accommodate a new way of life.

Though we are nine years separated in age and had spent much of our lives pursuing very different activities due to that age difference, I knew that David was a hard worker—a full immersion person himself. Those initial months of rehabilitation were stressful and demanding, but through God's empowerment and grace, my mother's determination, and David's own willpower, he continued to pursue his dream of being a physician. He had the strength of character and the full immersion qualities that enabled him to start again though under much more challenging conditions.

My father merely shook his head and said of his son, "He'll never amount to anything now."

I can only imagine how tragically painful his declaration must have been to my mother.

But despite my father's dour prediction—and against all odds—in the late spring of 1970 David returned to college, initially as a homebound student, to complete his last semester and was accepted into Michigan State University's College of Human Medicine. With the support of a personal aide, fellow students, supportive professors, our mother, and myself, he completed the requirements for his medical degree, only six months delayed from his initial goal.

It takes a village? Yes, it had taken a village to get David to that point. For the next thirty years, he was a practicing physical medicine and rehabilitation doctor in Ohio, Pennsylvania, Oklahoma, and Missouri. His patients included people with spinal cord injuries like his own, people who had experienced a stroke or traumatic brain injury, and seniors recovering from joint surgeries. His treatment recommendations carried with them a deep, personal knowledge and relatability—his testimony was profound, and his impact as a role model for his patients, undeniable.

Despite my father's demoralizing and dismissive statement, my brother's dream—and my mother's—was realized.

FIVE

WONDERING

My father did not live to see my brother disprove his condemnation that he'd "never amount to anything now." My father died on March 17, 1978, from a massive heart attack. Diabetes, heart disease, smoking, years of unacknowledged and unaddressed physical and mental issues converged to end his life at the age of fifty-six.

It was a sad, unnecessary loss of a life that began with so much potential. I wonder what our lives could have been had my father been able to have a healthy body and mind.

Walter Kent, my father, was a very intelligent man. I wish that I had known the man I believe he must have been before so much of his mind was consumed by illness. What might have been so different for me had this not taken place?

Sadly, I can only wonder.

I wonder if he would have told me stories of his World War II navy service, of being stationed in Singapore, or of swimming with the dolphins in the Pacific.

Would he have ever given me an indication about what it

was like to come home, marry, have two children, and build a life?

I wonder how he felt about his sister, his two half sisters, and his two half brothers. Or what he knew to be true about life, death, and all that comes between. Did he like being an engineer or, later in life, a parts salesman? Did he smile easily? Some early pictures I have seen tell me yes. What made him laugh? Why did schizophrenia have to take that away?

The few activities we tried to do as a "normal" family usually did not end well. Some were aborted midstream to keep them from being more painful than need be.

For example, we tried renting a cottage on Lake Michigan for a week one summer. Another summer we rented a camper. Neither attempts went well. We tried archery but the equipment became the focus, not the experience or the fun. We tried until my mom gave up the struggle of bearing fault for failures my father helped to create. He seemed to prefer sitting in the corner of our den with a *Time* or *Newsweek* magazine and his cigars. As time passed, he sank deeper into darkness, often shattering the silence in our house by an abrupt outburst of rage, slamming his fist against a wall with a bang. My memories of my quiet study time being sharply interrupted by these sudden behaviors make me recall the way I felt: powerless and anxious.

The instability and unpredictability of my home life during so much of my childhood and adolescence created in me a generalized PTSD response to the world. In attempting to cope, I gained a lot of weight (granted, my mom was raised with food as a reward—remember the banana splits?—and therefore used food as a parenting tool). As a result, I lost even more self-esteem as the kids in school made fun of me. Middle school and the first years of high school were not happy ones. I still today bear many of the emotional scars from those years.

I wonder how it would have felt to enjoy those years.

One of the most impactful personal challenges for me was having to begin middle school on my own as David had been injured about ten days before the beginning of the school year. I remember feeling afraid, anxious, and alone. My biggest nemesis turned out to be that stupid locker combination, of all things!

I wonder how different my experiences might have been without the added stress of having to face them all by myself.

David spent days in the ICU before being moved to a hospital room. There he spent weeks allowing the bones to heal as best they could. Physical therapy began as passive, small movements and rotations to improve circulation. After several months he was relocated to Mary Free Bed Rehabilitation Hospital to continue the work of gaining strength.

During these months, my mom and I were his constant companions and support. My father was not a participant—not that any of us expected him to be, particularly after a powerful altercation we had in our driveway.

My parents and I were coming home after being at the rehab center with my brother. My father had made multiple negative comments about David. When we arrived at home, my mother got out of the car and slammed the door so hard the car rocked. My father got out of the car, ran around the front to get in my mother's face, and yelled, "I ought to kill you!" Her response was "Go ahead!" Probably shocked back to his senses by her bold retort, he got back in the car and pulled into the garage as my mother stormed into the house.

This may have been the last interaction they had for a very long time. I often wondered at the time where her strength came from to say and do what she did in the driveway that evening. As an adult, I understand righteous anger.

Looking back on scenarios like these—all of which contributed to the formation of my perceptions of the world, my place in it, and my sense of self—causes me to wonder why I am a reasonably normal (debatable, I suppose), loving, productive human being today. Divine intervention, for sure!

And we know that all things work together for good to those who love God, to those who are the called according to His purpose.
(*Romans 8:28* NKJV)

SIX

YOU HAVE A DAUGHTER TOO

My mother was so determined that David would go to medical school and become a practicing physician that she often took on the persona of a mother bear protecting her injured cub.

I don't think she realized how "full immersion" she had become in this sole purpose and focus of her life. Looking back, I wonder if she was doing exactly what I have done much of my life: pursue success with a vengeance to disprove the negative expectations of others.

David was damaged, physically changed for the rest of his life. His obvious limitation now was his broken, unresponsive limbs. But aren't we all damaged in some way? For the rest of us, damage is internal, manifested in the choices we make. My damage, or challenge, was a lack of self-confidence, which undermined every interaction I had in the twelve short years of my life. Now, with the all-consuming nature of my brother's needs, I became the invisible child.

"You have a daughter too," I said quietly to my mother

standing in the kitchen one afternoon after a particularly long week. I was making dinner, and she had just come home from work. We had spent so many long hours with David in the hospital and rehabilitation center over the past weeks and months, and when she announced that we would leave for the rehab facility as soon as dinner was done, I'd said I did not want to go. She did not understand that. She simply expected that I would be there with her, supporting her. I was always the stand-in support.

Even today I can remember the expression of surprise on her face. Maybe she felt surprised at the idea that she had not been available to me. Perhaps she was surprised that I felt that way, having assumed I would be as enmeshed as she was in David's struggles, without realizing that I was going through my own trials. Perhaps I was invisible to my mother because I was not a project.

At the same time as I struggled to be visible to my mother, the measure of my value to my father was the level of success I attained in school. I vividly recall being asked by my mother to show my report card to my dad. Against my better judgment, I did. His only remark to me over a grade card full of As with one B was, "Why a B?"

One super cold, snowy day, my mother asked my father to pick me up at school so that I wouldn't have to walk all the way home. He was complaining when I got in the car about his clean car that was now covered with snow and salt because he had to come and get me. Evidently this ugly weather and now the condition of his vehicle were my fault.

This continued until I got fed up and told him to pull over and I would walk the remainder of the distance home. He did

—and so I did. Yes, an argument between my parents ensued later that evening, but I stood my ground, asserted myself, for the first time in my life. It would not be the last.

My father became unable to relate to the world, and certainly to us as a family. He never seemed satisfied with anything and was easily angered by most things, from the way the grass was mowed (we had a lawn service) to the lack of cleanliness of the cars. I slowly distanced myself from him and became a stronger, more independent person, a more verbal and more determined person, eventually making a conscious decision, at about sixteen years old, not to be a victim any longer, discontinuing all but absolutely essential interactions with my father.

Even though my father was not a positive participant in my life, he was a powerful force, becoming my motivation to be the best I could be, not only in spite of him but to spite him. "I'll show you who is able to succeed" became a constant mantra in my mind, a looping internal dialogue.

And I threw myself into that mission with everything I had. I taught myself to cook and bake with recipes my grandma used and my mom enjoyed. I did laundry and housework and gave the best effort possible to my schoolwork, earning a high enough GPA to maintain a place on the honor roll. I added a part-time job to my routine, saving all my earnings from this and babysitting for college.

One day it dawned on me that when I overachieved, I had a role, an identity.

I felt more important.

I wasn't invisible anymore.

For we are God's masterpiece. He has created us anew in Christ Jesus, so we can do the good things he planned for us long ago.

(*Ephesians* 2:10 *NIV*)

SEVEN

UNINTENDED CONSEQUENCES

Whom we become as adults is intertwined with and impacted by the people, experiences, and emotional connections we have made. I know God has a purpose for everything He allows to come into our lives, but sometimes His reasons for these experiences remain unclear. I am currently still wondering about several of these explanations.

My father provided no support to my mother without being given an itemized list of what he needed to contribute each month. At first glance we looked like a two-income family. Not in reality. For this reason I was not eligible for financial aid for college. Fortunately, I had been saving all the earnings from babysitting, a Saturday housecleaning job for an elderly neighbor, and my after-school job at the osteopathic hospital just a few blocks from our house. Over the course of about eighteen months, I demonstrated the character and work ethic my supervisors appreciated and was offered a full-time job at the hospital my senior year.

I attended class early in the mornings and went to work from 10:30 a.m. to 7:00 p.m. five days a week. In addition, I was always on call for my brother's needs as my mom worked all day as an executive secretary. She had been very relieved when, the previous year, I turned sixteen and could drive. During my high school years, I was David's driver to appointments and his overall transportation—in a Chevrolet passenger van adapted with a wheelchair side door lift. I can only imagine the sight we were on the highway . . . this little girl (I am only five feet tall now) at the wheel of this huge van. But in fact it was easier to drive a large vehicle than other smaller ones as I could see better over the dashboard and hood! I became an excellent driver, particularly because my mom spent hours with me as I practiced driving in the shopping mall parking lots on Sunday afternoons. Since the stores closed on Sundays, light poles, potholes, and the occasional passerby were the only obstacles as we drove round and round, circle after circle.

Unintended consequences? Despite the scarcity of exceptional role models but with lots of on-the-job training on so many levels, I had become a reliable, responsible student, employee, and adult, though too soon. Full immersion? Definitely! Striving for perfection? Undeniably! But why?

To prove my father wrong?

To make my mother proud?

To show my brother I could?

To have personal power, that self-esteem I failed to get from relationships at home?

To compensate for being shy, overweight, short, a girl?

To excel at something uniquely my own?

In retrospect, probably all of the above.

*Study to show thyself approved unto God, a workman that
needeth not to be ashamed, rightly dividing the word of truth.*

(2 *Timothy* 2:15 KJ21)

EIGHT

My mom was raised with a Christian faith and in the Baptist church. My maternal grandparents, particularly my grandmother, believed in salvation, baptism, church participation, and demonstrating that life to others in witness. I am not at all certain what my father believed, and for a very long time we attended no church at all.

Then, in some unique bargaining meeting between my parents, we started attending a neighborhood Presbyterian church. My father participated for a while, then gradually stopped.

My mom did her best to keep my brother and me on "her team," requiring us to attend church each week. This worked for a while, but then my brother began working late shifts at Blodgett Hospital, making it a challenge to keep attending the early morning service. Before long only Mom and I were attending church on Sundays. Missing the traditions she'd grown used to as a child, Mom returned to her home church, Calvary Baptist Church, and took me with her.

I never really connected seriously with the concept of salvation in my own life, although my mother tried, until I was a sophomore in high school. Campus Crusade for Christ had established a group of students at my school. They were using the auditorium to host a Christian magician's program. Someone stopped me on my way to class to offer me a ticket to come see André Kole's performance. I agreed. His performance was amazing and his testimony, profound.

I went forward at the invitation to talk with a fellow student about my own personal salvation. Two of my fellow classmates spoke with me, prayed with me, and I accepted Christ on the hallway steps that evening.

When I told my mother, she hugged me and cried, "Oh, honey, I am so happy!" She was obviously relieved to know of my decision, although I suspected she'd hoped to be the one whose testimony changed my life. I was fifteen. It would be several years before my brother would make a similar decision to follow Jesus.

The impact of this decision has been lifelong in more than the anticipated spiritual ways. I chose to attend both Grand Rapids Baptist College (now Cornerstone University) and Calvin College with the goal of teaching. In 1979, with a BA from Cornerstone and a BS from Calvin, both in education, I started my classroom career in a small church-owned school in Toledo, Ohio, the fall of that same year. I returned to Grand Rapids the following year and was invited to teach for Grand Rapids Baptist Academy (now NorthPointe Christian). During the next several years, while teaching first, second, and third grade classes, I completed a master's degree program in reading. With my desire to expand my teaching credentials further, I began course work to earn a certification in special education, with an emphasis on learning disabilities. I had completed all the credits for this license except for the final student teaching experience when my focus was redirected.

Being on call to support my brother placed my goals on hold at several points in my career.

In the spring of 1991, I ended up moving with David to Edmond, Oklahoma. The initial plan was to help him for a few months, perhaps one year, as he settled in. I ultimately stayed for nine years! During some of this time, I worked when I could tutoring and as a homebound/homeschool teacher for the local public school district. I was able to minister to students who were unable to attend school due to medical issues, pregnancy, or legal challenges. One of the young men I tutored was under house arrest for being the driver of an automobile causing the accident in which his best friend was killed. The reality of this burden he had to carry for the rest of his life was beginning to weigh on him. I felt a responsibility to provide more than just academic support, though my words had to be chosen carefully so as not to overstep my place as a public school (i.e., not Christian) educator.

God has a perfect perspective on everything we experience. He sees our lives from beginning to end and is never caught off guard by the things that blindside us. Growth and change are often painful, but nothing is as painful as staying stuck somewhere you don't belong. Growth and change bring uncertainty but also opportunity if we choose to see it.

As many of us experience, with changing life roles we have new challenges. Adapting to my alternating roles as daughter/sister, learner/teacher, and caregiver required me to suspend my needs, often placing them on hold for a later date. My years in Oklahoma were filled with circumstances that taught me a great deal about myself. Some of it I would have rather not acknowledged. I struggled with my identity: I was David's sister, his aide, his bookkeeper, his housekeeper, his driver. Even long-distance, as she remained in Grand Rapids, I was my mother's emotional support, her daughter, the sister she never had, her best friend. I had a part-time life as a teacher. I struggled with self-esteem issues, body image issues, control issues, and anger. I was angry at my father for his failures, my brother for getting hurt and changing all of our lives, my mother for choosing to put me last, relegating me to the "sacrificial lamb" and to the back-burner servant role, and not protecting me from the stressful, unpredictable environment I lived in as a child and adolescent.

The expectations of my mom to meet her emotional needs were draining. I loved her but was often grateful for the eight hundred miles that existed between Grand Rapids, Michigan, and Edmond, Oklahoma. I could deal with visits . . . of limited duration, focused on an event or celebration. I would be in the middle again but only for a short time; then I could regain my personal space and what little control I had over my world. Compounding these stressors was guilt because of feelings I was "not supposed to feel."

A coping mechanism in my house had been food. (Remember the banana splits?) I was so overweight by my teen years and so weary of how I felt about myself. Food helped me to stuff down and temporarily suppress emotions, but the extra calories generated their own emotional baggage later.

Fortunately, I lost a great deal of weight after I started my first job in high school and continued gradually to manage my size more adeptly over the next decade. I never really made peace with the hurts and the pressures of those formative years, however, and so always had a love-hate relationship with food.

The adult responsibilities I assumed at twelve years of age, the lack of a solid emotional foundation on which to build a stable adolescence, and the unpredictability of detours in my path due to my family's needs continued to stir up my anxiety and insecurities with a vengeance. I found myself again striving to gain control over something in my life. Food became that something. I read about others in the same struggle and what they did to "win." I practiced some of their strategies, such as anorexia and bulimia, which seemed for a time to be useful. I could control food rather than food controlling me. At least it felt that way for a while. I felt powerful for a brief time and then utterly hopeless in a repetitive cycle of struggle for control.

In hindsight, I believe God used this season to develop an empathy and compassion for people who suffer from compulsive and addictive behaviors . . . alcohol, smoking, drugs, whatever it is. I understand far more deeply the power these things exert and how they masquerade as solutions to life's traumas, temporarily empowering, until the ravages of a body overstressed and depleted appear.

When my mother began to have struggles with self-care, and it became clear that she could no longer be alone, her living with us in Oklahoma would soon become a reality. Once again my life would change. Once again I was the person who had to step up and be there. David would continue his life as it had been, but mine would change. More responsibility was coming to me. I loved her and truly wanted to do what was necessary and right for her, but so many emotions filled my mind and I feared what was ahead both for my mother and for me.

My salvation decision at the age of fifteen certainly changed my spiritual life as one would expect; however, it impacted my life choices and behaviors equally so. The sacrifices I was called upon to make, because they were best for others, were certainly ordained by God and inspired and empowered by Christ—not of my strength.

For by grace are ye saved through faith; and that not of yourselves: it is a gift of God: Not of works, lest any man should boast. (Ephesians 2:8–9)

O keep my soul, and deliver me: let me not be ashamed; for I put my trust in thee. Let integrity and uprightness preserve me; for I wait on thee. (Psalm 25:20–21)

The LORD is my strength and my shield. (Psalm 28:7)

NINE

THE REALITY OF FORGIVENESS

As I prepared for Mom's arrival, moving my things out of the way to make room for hers, I felt overwhelmed by the challenge I was taking on.

I found myself immersed in feelings I prayed I could somehow release.

Sadness. Frustration. Fear. Anger.

I spent so much of my life as the "invisible child," caught in the middle either between my mother and my father or between my mother and my brother. Now, with her coming to move in with my brother and me, I was preparing to be back in the middle—serving everyone's needs but my own—and invisible.

Again.

I asked myself, *How can I care for both my brother* and *my mother? How will I do this?*

I felt anxious and desperate at the very thought, and without an extra room for her, she would be sharing space with me.

For so much of my life, my mother had chosen David over me, leaving me to deal with my father alone. I never felt safe for long, and it seemed as though she was not there to protect me.

And now, preparing for her arrival, I suddenly realized how angry and resentful I still was over the choices she had made—and her ongoing expectation that I would be there to do whatever was needed to support her.

The reality of my world had been to be on call for my brother and my mother. While she had remained in Michigan and David and I were in Oklahoma, there had been "safety in distance." I had a small measure of freedom even though I was living in David's house to assist him.

Now she was moving in—and I was once again in the middle. Knowing she *had* to have help, realizing that her dementia made this a necessity—the decision was not hers—made me feel small and disappointed in myself for feeling the way I did.

How could I forgive her, make peace with the past, and fulfill my family duties?

How could I *not*?

I felt like I had no choice. I also felt like I had no clue even how to begin to forgive.

How had I even gotten in this situation? I realized it had started ten years before, in 1990, when David had needed my help. Again.

David and his first wife had been living in York, Pennsylvania, when their marriage began to crumble. David asked me to spend one summer at his house while his wife was in Hawaii for an internship in a law practice. She had just completed her law degree, and this was a great opportunity for her, although my sense during those months was that she was not coming back.

Indeed, the following spring I found myself, as I mentioned earlier, helping move David to Oklahoma City for his new job in physical medicine and rehabilitation at the University of Oklahoma. I resigned from my teaching position, packed up my things, put my car on a transport, said good-bye to my mom, and flew from Grand Rapids, Michigan, to York, Pennsylvania. David, his aide, and I set out driving to Oklahoma. He needed to have his wheelchair-adapted van with him there, so driving seemed the best option, as flying with a wheelchair-bound individual is fraught with many challenges.

When he asked for my help, I agreed to stay for a few months, maybe for a year. It ended up being nine years. Granted, I was much younger then, so it was easier to be that full immersion "doer"! The thought of doing these things now is overwhelming to me. Truly God provides the strength for what we are called to do (2 Corinthians 12:9–10).

During the next months of getting settled in Edmond, David established his medical practice and I built contacts in the local school district, which led me to working in their high school homebound program. I also tutored a group of neighborhood kids, after word spread that I was a teacher.

We were developing a routine and becoming more familiar with our new environment—scorpions (sitting under a pile of wet towels on the laundry room floor), snakes (lying on the crossbars of the garage door), and armadillos (running across the street—hilarious!) included.

Edmond, fifteen miles north of Oklahoma City, was small and friendly, with one quaint downtown main street in the style of the Old West. Small shops and businesses lined each side of the street, welcoming you to come in and visit. I realized without a doubt that we were truly in the West when, sitting at a traffic light one afternoon, a white pickup truck pulled up behind me. The driver wore a cowboy hat and western shirt, had a rope hanging from the back window, and large steer horns attached to the front grill! He made a lasting impression on me, for sure.

As did the young lady in the grocery store checkout lane who looked at me oddly and said, "You are not from around here, are you?"

I replied, "No, I'm from Michigan. Why do you ask?"

She answered, "You have an accent." This was news to me.

I talked with Mom frequently, and several times each year, for nearly a decade, David and I flew her from Grand Rapids to visit us in Oklahoma to celebrate birthdays and holidays, until it became apparent that she was not as independent as she had been. I began to worry that she might not be as adept or safe traveling alone.

Bless her heart, she had continued to work full-time but was beginning to feel less confident in her ability to keep doing this. David and I encouraged her, at age seventy, to retire from the accounts receivable position she had held for many years at the Christian Reformed Board of Publications offices in Grand Rapids, Michigan.

She seemed to enjoy the freedom retirement allowed. Then we started seeing changes in her. Perhaps the lack of a structured work routine, or the loneliness of being without her children, began to influence her cognitive abilities.

I remember her saying to me on the phone one day, "Things just don't work for me the way they used to."

I did not realize just how difficult simple living tasks had become for her. Had I known that she was already experiencing symptoms of Alzheimer's, I would have grappled sooner with bringing her to me in Oklahoma. However, this would not have made the reality much easier to manage.

The dilemma for me was that I was stuck. David depended on me, and now I was concerned that Mom was unable to care for herself.

It was about a year after her retirement that she began to call me with odd questions, such as "How do you turn the oven on?" When I received a call from a dear friend of hers, Cele, saying Mom had been in a minor car accident in the parking lot of the grocery store, I told David about these worsening struggles and reminded him that she would be more open to coming for a visit than to coming to stay. We agreed to get help for her in making this trip, so I called and asked Cele if she could help her pack things for a "visit to see the kids," lock up her condo, and fly with her to Milwaukee, getting her on the correct flight to Oklahoma City.

At this point Mom did not know that she was staying, not just visiting with us. I knew that she would not want to live in Oklahoma permanently, so this conversation would have to take place at a later date. For now I just needed to get all of us in one city so I could manage the situation. I was in the middle once again, mediator between Mom and David.

It was not until much later that I learned of the depth of the struggles she had been experiencing, alone and afraid.

Dementia steals the mind's ability to remember, perceive reality, process information, and problem-solve. She had been having difficulty writing checks and balancing her bank account. She had mistakenly overdosed on a medication, taking a double dose because she had forgotten that she had taken it earlier. Cele shared that she panicked and drank apple cider vinegar to make herself sick enough to empty her stomach.

She had experienced hallucinations about a man trying to break into the house and someone else being in the house with her, when in reality there was no one there. I can only imagine how terrifying all this must have been for her.

Mom was so happy to see us when her flight arrived. She was ready to enjoy being with her kids and, I am sure, ready not to be so far away and alone. So many times over the years she had asked David if he could move back to Grand Rapids. She wanted us all together. David had no desire to do this. On the contrary, he had been determined to escape my father in earlier years and perceived home as less than desirable. He had spent years trying to build a life away from the place that, because of our father's mental decline, created so much sadness. In spite of his physical disability, David managed to distance himself, to take flight. In a strange way, he and I had this in common but for varied reasons and in different ways.

Soon after Mom's arrival, the challenges and frustrations associated with our limited space, which we had managed to deal with in every previous visit, became more evident. Caring for a person with quadriplegia takes many forms with some of the very personal hygiene needs requiring a trained person much larger than myself. Being just five feet tall, I could not do everything for him, so a hired nighttime caregiver came each evening. After David was cared for, the caregiver slept in the bedroom adjacent to David's' room to hear him in the night if a need arose.

My bedroom was on the opposite side of the ranch-style house, and there was no additional bedroom space for Mom.

She slept on a love-seat sofa bed in the den and shared a bathroom with me. Lack of privacy was a substantial concern. Not ideal conditions. Short-term wasn't an issue, but long-term would be.

The challenges of caring for two people with such demanding needs felt overwhelming, even suffocating. I often wondered, *What do I do?*

I remember one of the conversations David and I had before Mom came, in which I expressed my concern about how to provide comfortable accommodations for her long-term. We discussed the possibility of assisted living or memory care services.

"David," I said, "we do not have an extra bedroom for her so that she can have some privacy, especially at night when the aide is here. She also needs medical support for her diabetes and asthma as well as constant supervision that I cannot provide all day every day."

David understood my concerns, yet his focus remained on his ability to continue his career. The challenges of meeting Mom's needs were going to be mine to overcome. I was angry with David. Angry about all the years of my life so impacted by his needs. Angry about things he could not control any more than I could. I had to forgive to let go so that I could take on what was to come. So the search began for the availability of senior care in our area. I located one facility close to our neighborhood, and upon visiting we both felt comfortable with the month-to-month arrangements they were willing to make considering our circumstances. We simply did not know enough to do anything but this. Introducing Mom to the idea of an alternative living arrangement would be difficult.

I waited for an appropriate opportunity and prayed for the right words to say.

One evening, as I was sitting in bed reading, Mom came in to begin her nighttime routine. I asked if we could talk about something. She sat down on the side of my bed, looked me straight in the face, and listened.

I remember thinking that she seemed very engaged and present. It was a surprising change from the often withdrawn, sullen, anxious, and depressed behavior I had seen intermittently and heard in phone conversations over the last several years. She had often seemed confused, disoriented, and lost, so unlike the person I knew my mother to be.

It struck me in that moment that Mom was here, sitting with me, making powerful eye contact, smiling. It was miraculous, quite frankly.

Carefully selecting my words, I explained that to provide her with more privacy, we would like her to consider having her own room in an assisted living home. She could be with us during the day and have her own private space at night.

Her response was a moment in time I will never forget.

She leaned forward, reached out for my hand, smiled, and said, "That's okay, honey. I'll do whatever I need to do to make things easier for you."

I was so surprised and relieved by this brief conversation. Sadly, it was to be the last one I ever had with my mom totally present and engaged. Had I known this, I would have made it last much longer.

We settled her into her room, setting up all the services (TV, phone, etc.) and nursing supervision she would need. Daily I planned out what David needed, determined what my student schedule looked like, and then called Mom to let her know when I would pick her up. When she knew I was coming, she would be waiting outside the door of the facility under the parking canopy. For a while this was a reasonably functional arrangement, but over time she began to perseverate on when we were all moving back to Grand Rapids.

On the drive back to the house, I had to be very creative with small talk to keep her mind engaged and focused on positive thoughts. She would ask me, "Have you talked to David about moving back to Grand Rapids?"

My response was always, "He has an important job here in Oklahoma and needs to be here for a while yet." I tried to refocus her to the idea that in the future we would go back, and with questions about how she was enjoying people in the facility, how her quiet time was going, how she wanted to help me that day.

As the days passed, she gradually became more detached, confused, and depressed, and sometimes experienced crying, angry outbursts. I often secretly felt I had betrayed her in taking her away from her home. I promised I would get her back to Grand Rapids as soon as I could, but for now I could not be in two places at one time. I wanted her to have a calmness in her spirit, that she would be going home, because that's what she wanted. She wanted all of us to go back home.

I had no idea how I would make this real for her anytime soon, but she needed something to hold on to that comforted her. All of us going home was that thing. The progression of her Alzheimer's led to personality and behavior changes, depression, anger, mood swings, disorientation, apathy, and irritability. The months ahead were going to demonstrate just how devastating this illness is. And I was not going to be able to give her what she wanted quickly enough.

One of her favorite hobbies, and the most calming activity for her now, was putting together jigsaw puzzles. This had been one of her favorite activities through the years. I would keep a folding table up in the family room with a puzzle for her to work on, key pieces in place to provide a scaffold for success. She gravitated toward it like it was familiar, comforting.

Mom had also been an avid reader but found reading too difficult now, so I tried to read aloud for her. She used to knit and crochet but could not coordinate these skills any longer. I suggested that perhaps we could get a latch hook rug kit, the kind we used to make together, but she did not think she could remember how to do it again.

On occasion she would be happy and engaged, wanting to help me fold laundry, sweep floors, work in the kitchen to prepare dinner. I often had to remind her of how to do the tasks she had taught me to do as a child some thirty-five years before.

One evening she wanted to help me clean up and load dinner dishes into the dishwasher. As we worked, I was reminded of the fact that when I was a kid, we did not have a dishwasher. That chore was mine. I hated washing dishes! I wondered if Mom would remember the time I disobeyed her by refusing to wash dishes and instead making a childish escape. Hoping to help her reconnect with the past, I asked her, "Do you remember when I ran away to avoid washing dishes?"

I think I was seven or eight at the time. She had taught my brother and me to be honest, respectful, and responsible, and to do what was right. We had chores to do each day, and for the most part I was okay with that. However, I did not like washing dishes and was determined on this occasion not to do them. My mother was not a pushover, so I waited until I thought I could sneak out, unnoticed. I got on my bike and rode away as fast as I could. My plan got me as far as my elementary school a few miles away.

Riding around the park adjacent to Mulick Park Elementary School, enjoying my freedom, I suddenly became aware that I was not alone. Glancing back over my shoulder, I caught a glimpse of a very familiar car. The driver I recognized as my mother, stern-faced and motioning me to "go home." She was also mouthing those words to me so there was no confusion on my part as to what her expectation was. I turned around and rode toward home as quickly as I had ridden away, with my mother following closely, matching my speed amazingly well.

The dishes were still in the sink, waiting for me to do my job. She said nothing to me but sat down with her crocheting at the kitchen table until my task was complete, lest I decided to test her again.

My bike was off limits for several days. I was grounded. There are consequences for choices. This was an effective lesson well learned, the impact remembered to this day.

I didn't see any recognition on her face of her recalling the event, but she looked at me and briefly smiled. Some basic maternal instinct was remembered. She may have felt what it was like to want to teach her child values, respect of self and others, the importance of making good choices and taking responsibility for those choices.

Watching her, the question of forgiveness for the past seemed so irrelevant to me now. I still had no answers, but my choice was clear. I asked myself, *Who is forgiveness really for?*

The reality is it frees us, the forgivers, of anger and stress, allowing us to move forward with hope and strength.

Over the coming months, I continued bringing up childhood memories, trying to help her make those connections.

"Mom, do you remember making candles in the basement on the little hot plate we had? We bought blocks of wax, colors, tools, and molds and created beautiful pieces of art."

"Do you remember Bootsie, our loving Boston Terrier, who would try to catch the Ping-Pong ball during games? She would run from one end of the table to the other jumping up to try to catch the ball. On one occasion, she actually did catch it! The look on her face was priceless. She was so astonished and had no idea what to do with the ball now."

"Mom, do you remember all the hours you spent helping me in my classroom, putting up bulletin boards with the lettering you spent hours at home in the evening after supper cutting out?"

"Do you remember all the Cabbage Patch dolls we collected? What fun we had in Toys "R" Us, selecting the exact dolls we needed to make our family complete, only to be back there again when the next new dolls came out."

"Mom, do you remember *The Sound of Music* and *South Pacific* we went to see so many times? Afterward we would go out to eat and share a banana split."

"Do you remember the game nights we had with our friends Bert and Opal, sitting by the fire after stuffing ourselves with homemade pizza? Bert always won the games. I wanted to be on his team every time!"

"Mom, do you remember those amazing rosebushes that grew up the walls of our old house? You were so talented in getting them to bloom every year."

Most often, she listened politely with a blank look. I think what I was really doing was trying to find her again, find something that would reconnect her to the person she had been. I longed for another moment like the one where she'd sat on the edge of my bed, so engaged and present, and told me she would do whatever she needed to do to make things easier for me. Looking back, her response seemed like an acknowledgment of sorts. It felt healing in a way I hadn't anticipated. She had validated, if ever so briefly, that she recognized the burdens that were mine to carry.

I wanted her back so we could have more meaningful conversations. More mom-and-daughter talks. More smiles and laughter.

During the years after my father died and while David was living in other cities, my mom and I grew in our ability to share. It had often been so difficult in the years before. I think she was often rigid because of the struggles with her relationship with my father, closing off her emotions to protect herself. David was so consumed with his own future (rightfully so, I believe) that he had stopped being there emotionally for her. In my way, I tried to be there but had to protect my emotional stability as well. For many years I just denied my anxiety, simply putting my focus on achievement.

She had been with us for nearly two years when the cold she struggled to overcome took a turn for the worse. Though not unusual for the phone to ring during the night or early in the morning whenever David had a patient in the hospital, since Mom had arrived we were always overly sensitive to the possibility of something taking place at any hour of the day.

When the phone rang early this particular morning, I had a strange feeling. It was one of the nurses from the assisted living facility letting us know that Mom had developed a high fever during the night and had been taken to OU Hospital in Edmond.

We hurried to get there as soon as we could and were directed to intensive care, then were met there by her physician. He said the tests that had been performed so far indicated pneumonia, so she would be on oxygen and antibiotics to see if her condition would improve.

She was sleeping when we entered her hospital room, but opened her eyes at the sound of my voice.

I said, "Hi, Mom. David and I are here. You just rest and get stronger."

She turned her head and looked at me, and I recall thinking I was not sure how much recognition there was. Her eyes, once clear and more green than gray, were now cloudy and more gray than green. I felt myself shiver with a sense that I might be seeing my mother beginning to let go of her earthly body.

We visited several times every day. Each day there was no improvement. On her third day in intensive care, her physician told us that he wanted to do a procedure to check her lungs in hopes of gaining a better idea of what might be wrong since she was not responding to treatments. David told me that he agreed with this, and so we gave our approval. Now we had to wait for the results of the procedure to know how to move forward.

I prayed, *Dear God, please help the doctors to have wisdom. Please renew Mom to a life she would want to live or bring her home to be with you. She is ready to be free of the physical body causing her pain and the fearful confusion of her mind.*

And again we waited.

Whether from the stress of the pneumonia or the procedure, the effects of the sedation, or the impact of it all, Mom
slipped into a coma. She was not responding to any of the
treatments and was becoming so bloated from the medications
administered to her that she was nearly unrecognizable as
Lorraine Kent, my mother.

None of the data provided by the tests and the machines
indicated that she was going to come out of it. David and I
were told that the respirator was keeping her alive but her
brain was essentially dead. We had another decision ahead,
one even more painful than the ones before.

But how do you do this? How do you choose to take away
the one thing that is keeping someone alive?

David and I talked about what we should do. With his
medical knowledge, he knew so much more than I did that
Mom was already gone. She would not wake up. She would
not speak, smile, or laugh. She would never be Mom again.

Communication in our family had never been easy.
Defenses always came up, emotions interrupted, making satisfying interactions so difficult that most of the time they were
not even attempted. But now, even the hope I had of changing
this pattern someday was gone. Making that decision to turn
off life support would take it away.

The decision to turn off life support changed everything.
She remained with us for just thirteen hours before being
called home to heaven on April 13, 1999.

I had never seen my brother cry before.

Oh, how painful to see a loved one in need and there is
nothing you can do for them. Yes, you pray! You ask God for
comfort for them, but for yourself as well. I am tremendously
grateful that God provides strength for what we are required

to do and peace in the knowledge that we did what was right. I just never thought she would leave us so soon. To this day I wish I could have made her last days more fulfilling for her . . . I tried. The reality of forgiveness? The reality of forgiveness is that we all need it. We all need to be willing to give and receive it.

One of the discipline methods my mom employed throughout my childhood was the silent treatment. You knew she was not happy with you because she would just not engage. This cold shoulder behavior was very effective, and I hated that!

Now she was forever silent.

What I would give to talk with her again.

Pleasant words are like a honeycomb, sweetness to the soul and health to the bones. (Proverbs 16:24 NKJV)

TEN

AUNT HELEN WAS RIGHT

One of the most powerful experiences in our lives is letting go of a loved one. It is intense and painful, and it feels as though it may never end.

Mom's death was intensified for me because I knew I had to keep my promise to take her back to her home.

Much work was still ahead of me. Arrangements were made through the funeral home to prepare her resting place in Grand Rapids. I contacted several of my mother's friends and Calvary Baptist Church to begin the process of planning a Celebration of Life gathering.

I made airline reservations for myself, set David up to be cared for while I was away, and gathered up what I needed to take with me. The funeral home had provided a letter of explanation for the airline if they questioned what I was carrying in my bag on the plane. Security was not as stringent as it is today, so no explanation was required.

Mercifully, the flight was unremarkable, save the unique scenario I was living through.

I thought about the fragmented pieces of my life and how they brought to mind the jigsaw puzzles Mom loved so much. Questions such as *Why me?* and *How can I do these things?* filled my thoughts. I knew what I had to do, what I promised to do, and prayed that God would strengthen me to complete what lay ahead. The thought struck me that here I was, carrying my mother's ashes, in a small brown box, in a carry-on bag, to her final resting place.

Who does that? Me, I do that. Through the grace of God, living intentionally, with full immersion—not by choice but out of necessity—I did that.

Cele, the very dear friend who had been so instrumental in making sure Mom was safely received into my care in Oklahoma, again became a tool used of God in my life. She insisted on accompanying me to the cemetery the day after I arrived, not wanting me to be there alone. On Saturday morning she picked me up from the condo Mom and I had shared a decade before. We spoke about so many things. Her words, her voice were so comforting.

She said, "Nancy, I loved your mom. She and I were coworkers, but more than this, close friends. Lorraine told me how much she loved you and David and how proud of you she was. You were her pride and joy. I know how grateful she was for all that you did for David all these years. She wants you to be happy."

The day was warm, the sun bright, with a breeze that was soft and gentle. The cemetery grounds were well manicured and quiet during this midmorning on a Saturday in late spring. In the distance two groundskeepers waited patiently for us to do what we had come to do so that they could complete their assignment.

I suppose I had been quite stoic about all of this, not allowing myself to feel, just pushing on, for the promise to take her home again had to be fulfilled. While I was standing in the cemetery, with Cele who knew exactly why I should not be at this place alone, beside a small hole dug neatly in the earth next to my father's grave and beneath their joint headstone, my resolve faded away.

Cele prayed aloud for Mom's eternal rest in our heavenly Father's arms and for David's and my peace in the days ahead.

As I bent down and gently placed the small brown box in the ground, *all* the pain became too overwhelming to contain any longer. The tears began to flow. Cele reached out to hold me so that I could let go—physically, emotionally, psychologically, and spiritually. The visceral act of releasing Mom to God felt so profoundly overwhelming that it released the accumulated, unaddressed emotions of a lifetime in me. We walked slowly, arm in arm, back to Cele's car. Our relationship had changed this morning, deepened so remarkably through unity of purpose, out of love for one woman, Lorraine Nellie Newland-Kent, her friend, my mother.

Emotionally drained, I spent the remainder of the day sitting at the dining room table paging through piles of papers, pictures, devotionals, scribbled sermon notes, and what looked like insignificant scraps of paper. I soon came to realize that Mom had been putting things in "safe places" but forgetting where those safe places were. Cleaning out her things was going to be a major investment of time and energy, neither of which I had in reserve.

That evening I attended Mom's Celebration of Life with friends and family at the church. I had not seen most of the folks in the room for a very long time, and some were new to me. For many years my mother did not have typical family relationships with anyone due to the volatile nature of my father's erratic behavior. After he passed in 1978, I had several brief interactions with our closest family members but not in any way to develop strong bonds. My Aunt Helen, my father's half sister seven years his junior, and several of my mom's friends and coworkers shared memories over some wonderful potluck favorites.

After our meal I had the opportunity to talk with so many sweet folks who shared their personal stories with me. Aunt Helen pulled me aside and asked if we could talk privately. We walked to a small classroom down the hall. She seemed to know exactly what she wanted to say, and I must admit I was surprised by her determination to say it.

She spoke to me about her belief that it was now "my time to have a life"—to let my brother make a life for himself so that I could pursue my goals. She told me, "You have given enough to the family and it is your turn to be happy. Your mother would want you to."

The look in her eyes and the strength of her hugs left an indelible impression that I carried back to Oklahoma hidden deep in my heart. I would have to return to Grand Rapids, again, in the months ahead to continue to search through the remnants of many decades of our family story, identifying the valuable pieces. Perhaps in doing so I would identify the next door opening, the next pieces in my story.

I heard you, Aunt Helen.

In the following months, I tried to manage the condo long-distance. This was made more difficult when the insurance company began to insist that an unoccupied property was a danger and informed me they were not sure they wanted to continue coverage. This was complicated by the fact that a few years prior an adjacent unit had become available and Mom had convinced David to purchase it as a rental property. In the back of her mind she had hoped that maybe someday he would move back to Grand Rapids and live in it. I don't believe David's intention was ever to return, yet the idea of a rental would appease Mom and provide some income to him.

In other words, I had two properties, eight hundred miles away, that I was monitoring in addition to David's home and needs in Oklahoma and my work with students from the local school district.

I returned to Grand Rapids when it was necessary (and possible) and tried to begin work on the clean-out process. As I did, Aunt Helen's words kept repeating in my mind. Being responsible now for three properties in two states was not my idea of having a happy life pursuing my goals.

I determined to renew conversations with David about changing the situation as soon as I returned to Oklahoma. Knowing that it would not be his choice to move, especially back to the hometown he purposely left behind, I began considering taking measures into my own hands. I believed God wanted me to return to Grand Rapids permanently, so gradually over the next few months I made plans to accomplish that.

David did not want to acknowledge my needs, as this necessitated a major adjustment in his way of life, so I did what I could to prepare his world to continue without my being physically present. I agreed to carry on long-distance what he still needed me to do, such as his bookkeeping.

On April 15, 2000, one year plus two days after Mom passed, I had moved much of what was mine from Oklahoma back into her condo in Grand Rapids. A new century had begun only a few short months before, ending what had become a formidable decade for me.

With so much ahead, some of which I could never have anticipated, I was starting anew, beginning a new chapter in my life. God had closed a door and opened a new one. It was up to me to pick up the pieces of what was and fit them into what was to come.

I heard you, Aunt Helen.

Over the next three months I waded through Mom's stuff, painstakingly handling every item in the condo to be certain nothing I threw away was valuable. Each piece of paper, note, card, magazine, and book had to be read, opened, or paged through lest a treasure be hidden inside and mistakenly discarded.

Mom's penchant for stockpiling was magnified in this smaller venue—the condo was much smaller than my childhood house had been—and each closet was filled to overflowing: books, jigsaw puzzles, acrostic and crossword puzzle books, games from my youth and from my classrooms, videotapes of movie musicals and Christian musicians such as Bill Gaither, cassette tapes of her favorite pastors (Charles Stanley out of Atlanta, one of the best), and photo albums.

The den had been filled with Cabbage Patch dolls (some brought back memories of purchasing them together, some I did not recognize) and stuffed animals, its closet with doll clothes and collectible accessories. Some of these I donated, some I sold to collectors, some I sold in a garage sale, and some I just gave up on and added to the dumpster. My neighbors joked about trying to get to the trash dumpster before me so there was still room for their items. If they waited until trash pickup day, I had already filled it. This happened multiple times!

I had left many of my things in moving boxes in the basement while I completed the reorganization of Mom's belongings. What a relief when I finally settled in and was ready to begin reaching out for opportunities around me.

In the following months, I tried many things I had never tried before: singing with the Sweet Adelines chorus, working in retail food sales, catering, restaurant management, and doing several other things. I met so many interesting people, and I learned a great deal about myself and who I truly wanted to be.

So much of my life had been spent "cloistered" as the family caregiver. In addition, I'd attended Christian universities and taught in Christian schools. Reaching beyond small Christian circles and learning about the world and its opportunities (and certainly challenges) was exhilarating, and at the same time somewhat scary.

I took a couple jobs simply out of curiosity to try some things I had never done before. As I shared earlier, I had struggled with my weight and self-esteem for much of my youth, so though I had dated, I was not involved in any serious relationships. I had moved beyond the years of my life when I would have considered social life a critical priority for well-being. Those years were spent in other responsibilities of caregiving, my own education, teaching, and more caregiving.

Now, at forty-three, here I was working for a caterer and finding myself meeting new people nearly every day, preparing and serving food in small in-home gatherings or large galas and wedding celebrations amid hundreds of guests. I got to see firsthand what these kinds of events looked and felt like.

My world suddenly presented me with a mixture of people, some truly interested in helping me make a new life for myself and others who were quite a rude awakening. Some were fascinated by me and the uniqueness of my life experiences, while others were simply lost in survival mode, players and users looking out solely for themselves.

I had never been noticed before for being attractive or cute —until now.

I vividly recall my surprise when I heard a man make a flattering comment about me to another man behind my back. Imagine how this felt after all these years! The physical transformation I had been experiencing over time was beginning to be translated into a social and interpersonal awakening of sorts.

It suddenly struck me that all the years I spent as a bystander—watching other people get to have lives while I could only imagine the adventures they were experiencing— were now over.

I started to say yes to life.

Most importantly, I began saying yes to being the main character in my own story, not simply a supporting cast member to others in their stories.

No more vicarious living for me!

DAVID and I had both made promises to our mother to make her happy and fulfill all her dreams, and we both had become resentful of her at times. She held on to us so tightly. It felt as though both of us were suffocating in our own ways, not because we did not love her or want her to be happy, but because we did want her to be happy and just could not seem to accomplish this without personal sacrifice. I know that I certainly felt that way, and in hindsight I believe my brother did too.

This may have been one of the factors contributing to his desire to escape home as a very young man—my father's worsening illness but also my mother's neediness. Yes, she was a strong woman, but her strength often came from leaning on us for support, me in particular.

I continued to take care of David's bookkeeping and aspects of his life I could manage long-distance. He decided that he wanted to rent, rather than sell, the condo he had purchased a few years before, again to make Mom happy. It was across the connecting courtyard, the end unit on the next building up the street from the condo I was now living in. Mom's utopia was having all of us back in Grand Rapids together . . . that was her dream. I think in the same way I promised to get her back home again, he committed to keeping that property.

To help him find a renter, I placed an ad in the *Grand Rapids Press*.

A man named Denny Koenig would read that ad. Only God knew the full impact this small action would have on my life.

In mid-January of 2002, response to the ad had been minimal, so I renewed it one last time for two more weeks. On Superbowl Sunday evening, February 3, my phone rang. The gentleman on the other end said his name was Denny and he wanted to inquire about the rental property advertised in the newspaper. He said that he had sold the house he owned with his ex-wife and needed a place to move into.

We set up a time to meet the next day so he could tour the condo.

When he arrived at the door, my first impression was that he seemed like a very nice man, polite, respectful, and punctual. Quite different from some of the people I had met over the last several months! I noticed that he was tall, but everyone is much taller than I am. He was nicely dressed, with well-groomed blonde hair sprinkled with gray, and with gray patches beginning at the temples.

His grey-green eyes looking at me intently as we spoke conveyed a sense of calm centeredness that only a mature heart can project. He smiled readily.

As we visited, I learned that he had been in the car business for twenty-nine years, the last thirteen of those as the general manager of a Toyota dealership. He and his wife had moved from Iowa to Michigan several years before so that he could accept a position as GM of the Toyota dealership in Grand Rapids. Their two grown sons remained in Iowa. Shortly after the move, they divorced, ending twenty-seven years of marriage. I can only imagine how devastating that must have been.

Our conversation moved from one thing to another and suddenly we became aware that we had been standing in the kitchen talking for two hours. Denny was very positive about the place and agreed to rent. A simple rental agreement I had created was signed. The move-in process began the next day, gradually, carload after carload.

Several days later he called me to ask if I would like to go to a movie with him. He had won two tickets through a drawing at his office and wanted me to join him.

I said yes without hesitation, but after I hung up I felt surprised at myself. Questions raced through my mind.

What have I done? I haven't had a date in so long. I don't even remember how to do this!

Those old self-doubts played once again in my head, but I had committed, I had accepted. I would go.

That evening was very cold, and snow fell lightly. Denny was such a polite gentleman, opening the car door and the movie theater door, holding my hand as we walked to and from the car so I did not slip on the wet pavement. I don't remember the name of the movie, but I remember feeling that my decision to come had been a good one.

After the movie, we visited an old-fashioned ice cream parlor and shared a sweet treat. Somehow I did not mind ice cream on that cold winter night!

We talked, laughed, and had a lovely time. I remember that he walked me to my door, only a few yards from his, thanked me for going with him, kissed me ever so gently, and wished me a good night's rest.

As I fell asleep that night, I remember thinking that Denny was one of the kindest, most considerate men I had ever met, and that getting to know him would be fun.

A few days later he came in to have lunch at the restaurant where I worked, and to ask me if I would be interested in seeing the house he was moving out of. He felt that I would enjoy seeing it and perhaps meeting his cat, Annie. I agreed that I would like to visit. He picked me up the next evening, and we drove through East Grand Rapids, a very old, prosperous area of Grand Rapids.

We turned down a tree-lined street with beautiful old homes on each side. Some of these were mansions or castles, in my mind. We pulled into a driveway. Before us rose up an old, classic Spanish two-story home. Its facade appeared to be stone, although it was dusk and becoming more difficult to see all the exterior details. The yard did not appear to be huge but an adequate setting for the home.

Denny unlocked a side door into the house and led me into the kitchen. It was largely empty save the beautiful, impressive Victorian stove on the inside wall. This thing was amazing, the kind of item you would likely see in a museum!

We walked into the living room, also impressive, with ornate crown molding, tall ceilings and windows, and a narrow, creaky stairwell nearby leading upstairs. Each room was special with details that true craftsmen used to include in their creations a hundred years ago.

Denny began to call out for Annie, his cat. He had let her stay in the familiar old house until he had totally moved out and was ready for her to come live in the condo. After a few minutes a lovely, slender white cat poked her head out from around a corner. She was shy and skittish, so all I got to say was a quick "hello" before she disappeared back around the corner. We would get to know each other better in the days to come.

Over the next few months, Denny and I spent more and more time together. We visited the old house on several occasions in the course of the moving process, as well as many of the sites in Grand Rapids that I had not seen in their updated versions yet.

Hometowns have ways of growing and changing over time, seeming to "morph" into entirely new spaces. We visited the church he had chosen to attend, theaters, museums, restaurants, and shopping malls entirely new or so redesigned I didn't recognize them.

I met some of the friends Denny had made in creating his life in Grand Rapids, and we had the joy of spending the Fourth of July, my birthday, on a boat on Lake Michigan watching the fireworks display. We were tied up to other boats, sharing food, beverages, and stories.

I learned a bit more about Denny on each one of our outings together, confirming what I already believed about him. He was genuine, humble, capable, and loyal. He was also committed to faith, to his friends, and to his new life, even having to overcome some very unexpected challenges.

He also cared about Annie, the shelter cat who had endured many changes in her sixteen years of life. They had ended up as sole survivors together. She was not sure about me at first but soon learned to trust me. Before I knew it, she turned her loyalty to me, becoming my cat. We all began spending more time together until I was in the rental condo with Denny and Annie more than in my own. I would walk across the courtyard in the evening to shower and sleep in my place.

One evening Denny asked me if I could stay rather than go back to my condo. We discussed the possibility of my doing that later in the week when my work schedule was not so demanding. Once again, the old self-doubts rose up, but I said yes.

It was the beginning of us. Denny and I and Annie were now an us—the Koenig three. Annie got her family back too!

The months ahead were busy for us. We were both working, getting to know one another better, and creating our life together. I continued to do what I had been doing for David, long-distance, and care for both condos. Denny and I discussed having only one home to manage, and since the condo that had belonged to my mother and me was only being used now for storage, it became the property to sell. David agreed to the arrangement we had, to Denny and me paying him rent for his condo and to my selling the other. A realtor friend of Denny's assisted us in accomplishing this. She was able to find a buyer fairly quickly. We moved all my family treasures from one condo to the other with the help of one very generous and strong friend, Randy. His only reward—a homemade meal. One of several as it turned out!

One of the many lessons learned during this time of my life was that I was not as young as I used to be, as the saying goes. As much as I enjoyed my work, the amount of physical labor in catering and food service is immense. I found myself physically challenged by this and began to consider what might be God's next opening door. This revealed itself through a phone call from a dear friend of mine and former colleague at NorthPointe Christian Schools.

Ann said, "Nancy, the middle and high school has an open position for a special education resource room teacher for the upcoming school year, if you are interested."

As miraculous as this was, even more amazing was that I applied and was hired contingent upon completing the last course in my learning disabilities certification—the one I had to put on hold to move to Edmond, Oklahoma, with David more than a decade before.

They were so gracious as to let me do this student teaching practicum while teaching that fall semester. I was blessed to be accepted back into the Calvin College special education post-grad degree program, so many years after I initially began, to complete this last requirement for licensing certification. This was essential to be duly certified to teach what I was being asked to teach.

Again, I could see God's hand at work!

THE DILEMMA for me in this was that no one was aware of my living situation over the past months since returning to Grand Rapids, and I was not certain how this would be received by the school leadership. Knowing that the expectations for staff members had been high during the previous years of my ministry with them, I shared this concern and feelings with Denny. His reaction was one I will always remember.

He said, "I was going to propose but thought it was too soon."

Knowing how I felt took the worry of "too soon" away. Before long we were in Kay Jewelers trying on engagement rings. When something is God's plan, He takes care of the details.

On the evening he selected to present me with the ring (which was a much larger version of the one I chose), we drove to one of our favorite places: Reeds Lake in East Grand Rapids.

As we walked around the park and the shore, the wonderful smells wafting from Rose's Restaurant just behind us on the dock brought to mind the fun meals we had had there, sometimes just the two of us and several times with friends.

We sat down on a bench close to the water's edge and talked about the future. In the course of the conversation, he pulled the box out of his pocket, opened it, and asked, "Will you marry me?"

Oh my, if Aunt Helen could see me now!

As I prepared to start a new job with middle and high school students and readied myself to return to the college course work routine, I was also preparing for my wedding. We had decided on Saturday, October 5, 2002. Curiously, some of my recent experiences in helping to cater wedding parties provided me a smidgen of insight into how one plans a wedding. The location, Calvary Baptist Church, Mom's home church, for sure. Wedding invitations of course included Aunt Helen and Uncle Jack!

Not long after the invitations were put in the mail, Aunt Helen called to invite Denny and me to their house for a family BBQ.

When we arrived at their home in Lake Odessa, we were welcomed immediately. Lake Odessa is a small, close-knit, quaint town in which Helen and Jack were fully involved. Jack, a well-known physician, was vital to the town's well-being. As important as the two of them were to this tiny community, they were surprisingly happy simply to be at home surrounded by family.

Aunt Helen was beside herself, beaming at me and hugging Denny. She was so happy that I had done what she suggested. It was indeed *my time.* I was with someone I could see she liked, and indeed, later that day she told me he was the nicest man she had met in a very long time. She said that my mother would be so happy and proud of me. I thought to myself that I did not have my mother there to approve but I did have Aunt Helen's approval, for sure!

As the school year began and my course work for my intership/practicum class began, I met the instructor for my program who taught our weekly evening class. Debra, a tall blonde woman who smiled readily, would be coming several times per month to observe and mentor me in my classroom as well.

Debra and I became friends as we spent a great deal of time together, after each one of her observation visits, just talking about life. I shared about my life experiences with caregiving and how I had come to be here in this place, doing what I was doing. I told her how I had moved back to Grand Rapids after the death of my mom to begin life anew, how I'd met Denny through an ad in the newspaper, and how he'd asked me to marry him. I also told her how I'd begun a new job necessitating that I complete the certification process and how in the midst of everything I was also working on arrangements for our October 5 wedding.

One day, in response to all my descriptions, Debra, who had been intently listening, looked at me with amazement and said, "Wow! You are certainly full immersion!"

I thought a lot about her words.

I'd never heard myself described in those words before, but the phrase resonated with me immediately. I had been identified by the qualities of my personality that I had possessed all my life but that had never been so aptly named before.

In retrospect, our conversations led me to wonder if this accomplished college professor, from a highly respected and well-known Christian college, admired me for being so intense and so determined to accomplish what I wanted to achieve, if she admired me for jumping in hook, line, and sinker, so the expression goes, even though I had been afraid many times.

Perhaps she recognized that I possessed a strength of character and faith in God to take risks—to do what scared me.

Perhaps she saw similarities between us.

Perhaps she identified herself as full immersion too.

Once again, God had brought another person into my life at a strategic place and time. Even with all the emotional baggage I carried from decades of caregiving, from a life of being caught in the middle, from running interference for my family, God was there. He had not abandoned me. He was fulfilling His plan for my life. Perfection was not required, but faith, trust, and willingness to try were.

Aunt Helen was right.

A man's heart plans his way, but the Lord directs his steps.
(Proverbs 16:9 NKJV)

Being confident of this very thing, that He who hath begun a
good work in you will perform it until the Day of Jesus Christ.
(Philippians 1:6 KJ21)

ELEVEN

MAKING IT HAPPEN

Reverend Billy Graham said, "God never takes away something from your life without replacing it with something better."

I know this to be true, but there have been many times in my life when I wondered when the "something better" would be showing up. And yet God's timing is always best!

As wedding preparations began, knowing that I had the blessing of Aunt Helen meant so much to me. In addition, the idea of connecting with extended family I'd never had the opportunity to know well was exciting.

My Uncle Bill and Uncle Bob were twins, brothers to Aunt Helen, half brothers to my father. Uncle Bob was badly injured in a car accident as a young man and so had some permanent physical challenges. Uncle Bill had been the driver of the car and took responsibility for supporting his brother throughout his life. The most amazing, and initially startling, observation I made when I first met Bill was how much he and my father resembled each other. Only half brothers, they looked strikingly alike. Genetics is a wondrous science, yet this was a painful reminder to me that the kind of man my father was and the kind of man my uncle was were vastly different, belying remarkable physical similarities. I was envious, really envious, that he had not been my father, a "dad" to me, as he seemed to be to his own children.

The idea of asking him to walk me down the aisle and give me away was fulfilling for many reasons. But it was easier thought than done, for many years had passed and my extended family was aging.

I called and spoke to Aunt Betty to let her know what I was hoping to ask. She told me quietly that Uncle Bill had been suffering from the debilitating effects of Alzheimer's for several years and was not sure how he would handle such an honor, though she suspected he would want to try.

She handed him the phone.

"Uncle Bill," I said when he came on the line, "I have a favor to ask. It would mean so much to me if you would walk with me down the aisle and give me away at my wedding."

He hesitated for a moment and replied, "Oh, Nancy, I would be honored to do that, but I don't know if I can. I might not be able to walk all the way."

In hopes of alleviating some fear, I said, "We will be there to support each other."

Again, a momentary hesitation, but then came, "All right, I will try."

He nearly turned me down because he didn't want to let me down. My uncle wanted to fulfill the role that my father never could. What an amazing joy!

I had only been to a few weddings in my life and had never been involved in planning one. Where do you start? Thank goodness for the contacts I had recently made while working with caterers and event planners.

I contacted a woman I'd worked with who had expertise in wedding cakes, and who also turned out to be a talented designer of floral arrangements, table decorations, and simple, elegant accents for the church auditorium. Denny and I met with her at her home, selected our cake flavors (carrot for one), topper, my bouquet, etc. What a blessing!

Word of mouth led us to two musicians, a vocalist and an organist, who invited us to audition them as they rehearsed in their home church. Another blessing! The wonderful ladies of my mom's home church, Calvary Baptist, helped me out with food and beverages, and gave me contact information for a talented young harpist (an additional blessing!). Pastor VanNorman was fabulous, leading Denny and me through some premarital counseling so that he knew we were well suited for each other. He agreed to officiate our ceremony, so we must have passed his course!

In our attempt to be as financially prudent as we could, Denny and I provided the labor for much of these preparations. I selected and sent out invitations, then purchased and created some of the table decorations.

The same philosophy carried me through shopping for my dress. Kathy, my friend who had also been a wonderful friend to my mom, accompanied me to find a dress suitable as a wedding dress, which was not an easy task considering our limited time frame and my small size (dresses for short women are not readily available).

We ended up in the formal wear section of Steketee's department store. Kathy, bless her heart, already had a dress, so it was up to me to find mine. I picked out two lovely floor-length dresses, one creamy beige with lace and the other a beautiful two-piece outfit, skirt and jacket, in navy blue. The first was lovely, but the second was the one. I tried it on and looked and felt like the woman I had always wanted to be: strong, sophisticated, classic, elegant. The only alteration was to shorten the skirt hem a couple inches. Kathy knew of a seamstress who could do this for me, and the purchase was made.

The next step was to locate a necklace that would serve two purposes: one was to be beautiful, but the most important was to hide the surgical scar at the base of my neck from the thyroid surgery I had over twenty years before. We went to Kay Jewelers, where Denny and I had purchased our rings, and I found a beautiful choker-style silver-and-gold necklace. I felt this would coordinate nicely with the earrings I already had. My plan was to wear the small gold angel lapel pin, in remembrance of my mom, and consider myself well dressed. All the accessories would blend with the silver pumps I had already purchased. My ensemble would also nicely blend with the decorations and cake, which were silver, gold, and navy.

Fortunately, Denny took on his part admirably. He arranged for tuxedos for himself as well as for Scott and Chris, his sons who drove in from Cedar Fall, Iowa. Gina, soon to become Scott's wife, already had a lovely navy-blue gown. Mary, Denny's mom, had a beautiful creamy golden-beige dress that was perfect for her. Aunt Betty, Uncle Bill's wife, wore a yellow-gold outfit that suited her very nicely as well. Aunt Helen, classy as always, wore a coordinated beige-suit-and-white-blouse ensemble. We had told these ladies the color palate, and they ran with it astoundingly well.

I remember thinking, when Denny and I compiled a list of

names and addresses for invitations, that we had quite an eclectic group of family, friends, coworkers, and neighbors covering four states. Denny had friends from his twenty-nine-year career in the car business, from his more recent work in the mortgage business, plus family and friends from Omaha, Nebraska, from Cedar Falls, Iowa, and locally from Grand Rapids.

I had family and friends, teacher colleagues, coworkers from catering, neighbors, and even a couple high school friends from decades ago. Many of my mom's coworkers and friends, neighbors from my childhood home, and my brother, David, who had moved from Oklahoma to Springfield, Missouri, all planned to attend. David was unable to come to the ceremony in the end (the reasons for this I learned later), but he called the evening before as we were beginning rehearsal. He was able to hear the organ in the sanctuary and remarked on how beautiful it sounded. He wished us the best for our special day.

As the date we had selected—Saturday, October 5, 2002—neared, we anxiously watched the weather forecasts. Michigan weather can be unpredictable, but God's hand blessed us with warmer-than-usual temperatures, sunshine, and only a gentle breeze.

For much of the day I was so preoccupied making sure that all our family guests were taken care of and those carrying out their tasks were ready, I had not even noticed the lovely weather until late in the afternoon when we were able to pose for pictures outside on the bridge walkway in front of the church.

Denny's mom, dad, and sister, who had arrived the day before, were situated at their hotel; Scott, Chris, and Gina were managing with limited accommodations (sleeping bags) in the basement of our condo; and the additional members of this "production" were beginning to fulfill their roles: the sanctuary was being decorated, the cake had arrived, the food preparation was moving forward. The musicians arrived and prepared to perform as we had arranged. Our photographer, who had arrived earlier in the day, orchestrated the wedding party, family groupings, and a special series of pictures with my aunt and uncles, which are treasures for me today as all those dear folks have passed.

Writing these memories prompted me to pull out our wedding album, and I was transported back in time to an intensely emotional journey, seeing all that took place through the photographer's lens. Often unnoticed, certainly unobtrusive, while memorializing my life-changing celebration, she made me feel so special. She captured not only the event but the emotions of the interactions, the smiles, the hugs, the laughter, and the occasional tears.

She was there when Uncle Bill was able to fulfill the hope of walking with me down the aisle.

She was there when Pastor Van Norman came to the "obey" part of my vows and I hesitated before responding, making the guests murmur and laugh at my honesty.

She was there when one of the candles Denny and I were to light together simply would not stay lit.

She was there when we exchanged rings and were pronounced husband and wife.

She caught the joy when we stood in the receiving line and greeted and hugged friends I had not seen in decades, and when Aunt Helen and I shared the moment, looking into each other's eyes, smiling, embracing, communicating that all-knowing validation that I had heard her and done what was right for my life.

What amazing roads my life has taken me down, my path crossing with those of inspirational, exceptionally caring individuals who had faith in God, love for each other, and room in their hearts for me—this "little" girl in so many ways, building a life of her own. Leaving behind the burden of caregiving, moving forward into God's next chapter for her life. I could only imagine at the time what the future would hold, but I trusted God for His continued guidance. He had brought me to this place, on this day, for a remarkable purpose.

Dr. Charles Stanley said, "Not only does adversity lead to spiritual maturity in this life, it purchases for us a crown for life in the next. God understands the trauma of dealing with adversity. He has not overlooked the sacrifices we are forced to make when adversity comes our way. Therefore, He has provided a special reward for those who 'persevere under trial.'"[1]

Be kindly affectioned one to another with brotherly love; in honour preferring one another . . . Rejoicing in hope; patient in tribulation; continuing instant in prayer. (Romans 12:10–12)

TWELVE

LEARNING CURVE

Saying "I do," exchanging vows, and cutting the cake were definitely the beginning of the new life I had said yes to and the beginning of my awareness of the enormity of the learning curve I was to encounter.

Our wedding day was truly amazing, and amazingly exhausting! The evening was slipping away as we finished helping break down tables and chairs, undecorating the auditorium, and gathering our belongings and wedding gifts.

Denny had reserved a beautiful room at the gorgeous Amway Grand Plaza Hotel in downtown Grand Rapids for that night, but by the time we arrived, we were so tired we slept like logs. Our breakfast the next morning was delicious, especially since neither of us had eaten much of our wedding meal. We were so engaged with our guests that eating was not the top priority.

That cool breeze and lovely warm sunshine of Saturday had become a cold wind overnight, and our plans to explore the newly renovated downtown area were abbreviated. We headed home to open wedding gifts, begin our thank-you notes, and start to organize our cherished memories and keepsakes from our special day.

The life we had begun together continued now as husband and wife. I returned to my classroom teaching and working on completing my degree, and Denny was building a new career in the mortgage industry.

How did Denny get here? After twenty-seven years of marriage his divorce was a traumatizing experience. I have witnessed what the mere consideration of divorce does to people, namely my parents, and I was a support system in the divorce process for my brother. I helped David's attorney to minimize some of the expenses and assisted in relocating my brother to an entirely new venue.

For Denny, the question became, how does one reconcile nearly three decades of marriage ending? How does one start over?

Denny made it a time of renewal for himself by resigning his position as GM of Toyota Grand Rapids, transitioning into the mortgage industry by learning everything he could about it, selling the old house, and using his solitude to soul-search and reevaluate his priorities. He knew that he wanted another relationship and made the choice to be with me. He was quite successful with all these endeavors, until the financial instability of the mortgage industry spiraled into a crisis.

I vividly recall the amount of stress he felt at this time, wondering what to do next. He thought he had made a wise choice leaving the burdens and stress of the GM position, believing the financial gain would be worth it. He did not know what conditions were about to change for the mortgage industry, ultimately leading to its functional demise. The economic climate in Michigan was stagnant, motivating us to consider moving somewhere with more potential for him. A recommendation from our close friend and strong furniture-moving buddy Randy, over dinner one evening (one of those promised homemade meals), led us to pursue the idea of Colorado Springs, Colorado. He said it was the most beautiful place he had ever lived.

During the winter of 2005, I began researching the possibilities for teaching positions in the Colorado Springs area. My search led me to respond to one school offering employment in the same type of work I had been doing over the past three years, middle school special education. I applied, and within a few days I was interviewed via telephone and hired the following day. Not knowing the area, the location of the school, or its student population, I was clueless about what was ahead of me. I was simply thrilled to have this open door, excited for a more hopeful business climate and employment opportunities for Denny.

In June of 2005, we flew to Colorado Springs to begin planning our move, locate a place to live, and learn more about the school that was offering to employ me. A dear sweet lady named Joan, an assistant principal of the school, drove us around so that we could become familiar with the city. We noticed that we would need to acclimate to the elevation, over six thousand feet, as well.

Our dear friend Randy had been accurate in his description of the beauty of this place. I could not stop staring at the mountains! Each day they seemed different, shadows just right so that the foothills, not visible the day before, suddenly appeared. The sunrises and sunsets were glorious, and the snowcapped peaks made me want to see them from the top.

One of the goals for our visit was to locate a place to live, a rental property until we had time to figure out where we wanted to be permanently. We looked at several rental homes listed in the local newspaper, and by the end of the week we were able to sign a lease on the closest house to my new school district. The house was small, not in the best of condition, but would do for what we needed temporarily. We now had the next step in our life together.

On a hot Saturday in July of 2005, we rented a Ryder truck and began to load our belongings. I had resigned my teaching position at NorthPointe Christian High School and said good-bye to students and colleagues. To my amazement several of my students and parents showed up to help us. We made huge strides that day, so much so that we could leave the next morning, Denny driving the truck and me driving our car, filled to the roof, with Annie, our sweet, old fur baby, hiding under the seat in the back, which is where she rode most of the way across the country.

We drove until dark and found a hotel for the night, beginning the next day to complete the long trip. Some of the scenery was beautiful, some simply cornfields and cows. When we arrived in Colorado Springs, the air conditioning in the rental house did not work, so we unloaded a little, then went to find a hotel room for the night. This was a huge challenge, as a major sports competition was going on in town and most of the hotels were full. I knew that as disheartening as this first experience was, God had a plan and was not leaving us to figure it all out on our own. Full immersion . . . yup! The strength that we needed was miraculously provided.

Once we settled into the house, I prepared to settle into my new classroom. As challenging as this was—setting up my entire room in a new school I had never seen and only having been in Colorado a few weeks—I tried to stay focused on the positive aspects of our new life here. The beautiful scenery, the less humid climate, the better economic opportunities for Denny, and certainly my blossoming friendship with Joan were pluses.

I now had my foot in the door of public education, though I felt like such an outsider in the school. Most of the staff had worked together and with many of the same students for years, so they continued to do what they did with and for each other. I never felt part of the group and struggled to establish myself in the school's "pecking order."

I confided my frustration to Joan after one of my students stole money out of my purse for the second time and the remainder of the class tried to bait me into saying something they could use against me. I was not prepared for this mind-set; it certainly seemed like "survival of the fittest" in a world I was unprepared to navigate. I managed to put up with the environment so foreign to me with little to no intervention from leadership (except for Joan) for six weeks.

By this point Denny was learning the insurance business and was in the process of gaining certain licenses. He had not had enough time to establish himself. I really could not quit, we needed the income, but I was very frustrated. Denny was so supportive, and we made the decision that I would resign, believing that God would take care of us.

I told Joan of my decision, and as sorry as she was to see me go, she understood. We sat for the longest time as she shared some of her personal experiences during her long career in education, and we grew even closer as friends. She offered to contact a friend, a young man whom she had mentored as he transitioned to school administration and who had moved to a different school district. She thought his contacts there might be beneficial to me.

Denny's statement of belief that God would take care of us was proven accurate as within a few days my phone rang. This friend of Joan's had become principal of a large middle school. He needed a special education resource room teacher for the seventh graders in his building. I met with him, toured his building (one of the nicest school buildings I had ever been in), and was told he would call me the next day. He did call the next day, but rather than schedule a more formal interview, he offered me the job!

Miraculously, I was unemployed for just two weeks. Not only did God provide another job, He allowed me to be in a much nicer building, with people who seemed to recognize my desire to serve them and the kids, and with students who seemed a better fit for me (and did not steal from me). He also provided an income that was greater than what the other district was paying me. God provided this as a stepping stone to the last move I would make in my teaching career, which was to Madison Elementary for the following year and for the next twelve after that. I had come full circle—back to where I began my teaching career in 1979, with the little people in grade school.

During the next several years, Denny grew in his knowledge of the various local insurance companies, gained his licenses, and became an independent agent, servicing seniors with their Medicare and other insurance needs. He loves what he does to this day.

We were able to purchase a house in 2007, which was still in its formative construction so we could make a few changes to the floor plan. Had we waited longer to buy, I would have lost so much of my investments in the stock market, so that when the recession came in 2008, we would not have had enough for the down payment.

God directed all of our circumstances to protect us from loss. I was blessed to become the interior designer for our new house, which was fun, exciting, scary, and expensive, but we have a home now to enjoy and be thankful for. It was definitely a team effort, and we learned much more about Colorado driving all over to purchase home furnishings.

I was also learning how to be a wife as well as an educator in the public school sector, how to accept help from a friend I'd known for just a few weeks, and how to trust God, again and still, for a future I could not see. The promises of God—to be with us (Isaiah 43:2), protect us (Psalm 121:7), strengthen us (Proverbs 18:10), provide for us (Jeremiah 29:11), love us (Jeremiah 31:3), and give us peace (John 14:27)—are reliable.

Despite my substantial learning curve, God knew what Denny and I needed before we did and answered our prayers for guidance, fulfilling every chapter in His plan for our story.

A story still in process.

As the saying goes, "You can't go back and change the beginning, but you can start where you are and change the ending."

And God is able to make all grace abound toward you; that ye, always having all sufficiency an all things, may abound to every good work. (2 Corinthians 9:8)

THIRTEEN

ZUCCHINI

If you have ever planted a vegetable garden, or you have friends who have, you have been on the giving or receiving end of zucchini. The plants are quite prolific.

My husband often comes home with gifts from his insurance clients. These have included cake, cookies, smoked meats, encouraging notes, gift cards, salsa, and pickles.

One day he came home with zucchini.

Not wanting to waste it, I began looking for a zucchini bread recipe. I love cookbooks—they speak to me. The last time we moved, my husband joked that he would divorce me if I added another cookbook to my massive collection. As I began to scan the titles on the shelves, a particular one titled *Stone Soup* caught my attention.

I opened the cover to see my Aunt Helen's signature, as this had been a gift to me at my mother's memorial service in 1999.

Aunt Helen has been gone many years now, having lost

her struggle with breast cancer in 2011. This made the rediscovery of her gift so special. Even more impactful was the fact that her handwritten recipe card for Amish Strawberry Salad was wrapped in my mother's handwritten recipe for the same item (must have been a good salad!).

Seeing their handwriting pulled me up short. These were both strong, capable women, and my heart was touched. My mom's death had brought me back to Grand Rapids, and Aunt Helen's encouragement had motivated me to stay.

And to think I got to experience this poignant moment of reflection because of a simple zucchini.

Intrigued, I glanced at the titles of the other cookbooks on my shelves. My thoughts traveled to how each of these treasures joined my library. Some came to me via church groups or school groups. Others featured regional specialties, like travelogues illustrated with photographs of culinary delights. Still others were gifts from friends and students.

What all my cookbooks have in common is that they are all connected to me by personal or generational history, relationships, and emotions. Such familiar names and so many childhood favorites!

What draws me to specific cookbooks? Sometimes the cover or title is captivating, as is the case with *The Little Red Barn Baking Book* by Adriana Rabinovich, *The Yellow Farmhouse Cookbook* by Christopher Kimball, *The Back in the Day Bakery Cookbook* by Cheryl and Griffith Day, and *The American Century Cookbook* by Jean Anderson. Sometimes the author is a well-trained culinary master like Jacques Pepin or a well-known celebrity like Julia Child, Martha Stewart, Ree Drummond, or Ina Garten. Sometimes the publisher is the key: Prentice Hall, Wiley, Good Housekeeping, Better Homes and Gardens, Betty Crocker, Reader's Digest, or the Food Network.

And the recipes reflect such creativity. Who thinks this stuff up? Pigs in a Blanket, Venison Sausage Slim Jims, Sloppy Joes, Chow Chow, Puppy Chow, Hush Puppies, Buckeyes, Snowballs, and Ambrosia.

Recipes provide rules to follow, structure to ensure the likelihood of success, lists of ingredients, ordered steps, helpful suggestions, and ideas for personalizing the outcome. Conceivably, perfection can be achieved if directions are followed accurately. Somehow this is enticing to me. The opportunity to create something with the potential to be perfect is a win-win, but you can still enjoy it even if it does not quite replicate the ideal.

Looking more closely, I noticed the preponderance of diner cookbooks I have. Fascinated as I am with the rich history these exemplify, I cherish them. They are culinary visits to the past, including decor representative of the culture and traditions of working people—Americana in culinary genre—the "blue plate specials" showcasing resilience and efficient use of resources, or rationed items, during WWII. I also noticed many Amish and early frontier (i.e., cowboy) titles boasting simple ingredients for recipes such as biscuits, stews, pies that provide extraordinary comfort. Yummy!

The zucchini bread was exceptionally satisfying due in part to its main ingredient being a gift and to my hours of total absorption in recipes, people, places, events, and the emotions attached to each of my cookbooks. Who could have imagined "full immersion" intensity inspired by zucchini?

For he satisfieth the longing soul, and filleth the hungry soul with goodness. (Psalm 107:9)

FOURTEEN

POWER OUTAGE

I don't deal well with electrical power outages.

Whenever the power goes dead, I instantly feel anxious and questions flood my mind:

What caused the outage?

Am I the only one affected?

How long will the power be off?

What-ifs always raise my blood pressure and drive me to pace the house restlessly, too distracted to focus on much of anything useful. Perhaps my discomfort stems from the lack of power and control I felt at so many stages of my young life.

I felt *powerless* as a child when my father controlled the environment by his unpredictability.

I felt *powerless* as a young person when my world changed the instant David's world changed and I became a key link in his chain of care.

I felt *powerless* beginning junior high (middle school) alone.

I felt *powerless* when my parents fought, and powerless in

the separation by walls and silence when they stopped speaking altogether.

I felt *powerless* when I tried to tell other kids why I couldn't invite them over to play at my house with my father there and my brother's hospital bed in the living room.

I felt *powerless* when my weight kept creeping up to the point of being obese and I could not get it to go down, when I knew society devalued and underestimated me because of my size.

I felt *powerless* when my mother served my father with divorce papers and I became his bargaining chip.

I felt *powerless* when I tried to be my own person and got a disappointment-driven accusation—"I thought you would support me in this!"—from my mother. I still remember the look on her face as she spat the words at me.

I felt *powerless* when I became caregiver to both my mother and my brother at the same time.

WHEN THE POWER returns to the house, my sense of relief is always intense. My anxiety abates. My blood pressure goes down. The routine of resetting clocks helps me regain a sense of normalcy and peace as power—so lacking throughout my childhood and adolescence—is reestablished.

I crave predictability in my world. There is comfort in an expected normal, a routine that makes sense and accomplishes important goals. To achieve this, I've come up with a number of strategies:

- Making lists
- Making schedules

- Making routines
- Developing long- and short-term goals
- Preparing for contingencies

AS PART of my need for personal control (and, yes, even perfection), I have come to realize that I am a sequential yet global thinker. I love part-to-whole processes. I am the most confident when I have at least some of the pieces and know what the final product should or could resemble. This may help to explain why I love jigsaw puzzles, recipes, and cookbooks. I am able to control the work and creatively, independently achieve the intended outcome. I do not work optimally being micromanaged. The locus of control is then external rather than internal. I need to finish what I start, and being interrupted too frequently frustrates me. Perhaps this is a manifestation of the intensity of focus of my full immersion personality.

I must make sense of the world. I look for symmetrical, balanced, coordinated, cohesive ideas, in books, music, television shows, and movies. I need a logical plot and a satisfying conclusion. Perhaps predictable equates to controllable in my experience. Some might consider this boring, but I see myself as solid, grounded, and responsible. My friends, family, students, and colleagues know what to expect from me, although I occasionally surprise everyone with a sweet treat or a silly new dance move.

I was fortunate to have a student several years ago who referred to as me as small and sassy: small package, powerful force. We both enjoyed our repartee, joking and poking fun with each other in a very special relationship. She provided me with a unique perspective on a piece of my personality I had never really identified. Having this charming, talented young lady in my class was an unexpected joy, heaven-sent to be sure.

Because of this need to have some personal power and control, I hold on to stuff—words, ideas, emotions, true friendships, and things. My role model for this behavior was my mother. Raised during the Great Depression and experiencing shortages and rationing, she kept things. When you were fortunate enough to have something, you managed the resource well. This pattern was evident in the house I grew up in by the additional refrigerator and chest freezer in the basement as well as by the number of closets everywhere, all filled with things: towels, sheets, blankets, pillows, clothing, shoes and boots, tablecloths, holiday decorations, "just-in-case" items. I loved the uniqueness of each one. Perhaps an abundance of things in closets represents power to me—the power of options, of choices, and the potential for needs to be met.

God has not given us a spirit of fear, but of power and of love and of a sound mind. (2 Timothy 1:7 NKJV)

FIFTEEN

CLOSETS

As a student of history, I am fascinated by the sheer volume of belongings we all have today in comparison to the minimalism of previous generations.

The pioneers who traveled in covered wagons during the westward expansion of our nation had to make what must have been heart-wrenching choices about what to take. To make matters worse, they often faced leaving treasured heirlooms along the trail as the challenges of the environment demanded a lighter load. Homes on the prairie were constructed with the sparse natural resources available and therefore were small, utilitarian, and lacking in storage space. Closets were unnecessary in the floor plan.

Fast-forward to today, when technologies, inventions, discoveries of the decades, even centuries, between then and now have given us "stuff" to want. We collect the "next big things" and need places to store them, building increasingly larger homes to accommodate our belongings or renting "extra" storage for all our "extra" stuff. Having "things" equates to choice, power, and control.

My childhood home was the perfect example of this phenomenon, being a two-story brick colonial with a huge basement, an attic, and plentiful spaces holding an abundance of treasures.

My favorite space was the closet in my bedroom. Though the smallest of the three bedrooms, my room offered a unique closet that was oddly configured to encompass the stairwell. My walk-in closet consisted of a hanging clothes rack, an overhead shelf, and a deep cabinet extending so far into the wall that I could not reach all the way to the back. Inside this cabinet were shelves that held the best of my dolls, puzzles, books, and drawing tools. The top of this cabinet was perfect for sitting, leaning back against the wall, and reading, drawing, or coloring. I loved it! I kept my personal "little girl" things in here. It offered me a cozy, safe space to be alone with my most cherished belongings.

When my brother moved on to college life and his bigger room became mine, I inherited two double-door closets. The initial challenge of deciding what to do with all this space seemed daunting, yet it took little time to determine how to utilize the room well. All my belongings had a home.

This room was next to the master with its own set of two double-door closets. I did not venture into the master space often except to put away clean linens, etc., but I did notice that my mother's closet always smelled like her perfume. Timeless, by Avon, was a favorite. Her classic suits were always color coordinated with a pocketbook, pillbox hat, high-heeled pumps, white gloves, necklace, and clip-on earrings. She wore the beautifully boxed, heavy nylons and garters that were the hosiery of her day.

My father's closet held dozens of white-shirt-and-tie combinations with dress slacks all neatly pressed. Belts were hung on one side. In a well-orchestrated ritual, he polished his shoes once per week on a wooden shoe-shining butler. The odd charade of his behavior was that he continued doing these things even when he stopped working. His daily strategy was to be shaved and fully dressed and to eat the breakfast my mother had fixed, all before she left for her job. As soon as she left, he would change out of his dress clothes, put his clean shirt in the laundry hamper for her to wash and iron. He might make one or two phone calls and sit in his recliner all day wearing a smirking grin. I interpreted this as satisfaction that he was getting away with something. He certainly was not giving his employer the appropriate effort. My mother knew nothing of this, putting me in an awkward position of having to tell her.

We both knew little of the things my father did during the day, or where he went when he did leave the house. He never let us into his world unless he needed something.

Early one winter evening, as I was fixing dinner and my mother was on her way home from work, the phone rang. My father was calling. Sounding shaken and humble, he asked us to come and pick him up. He'd had an accident. The company car he was driving was being towed.

When we arrived, it became clear that he had totaled the car. The fact that he was not injured or killed was miraculous. It took several months and several other strange events before we came to suspect that he had experienced a heart attack and lost control of the car.

I recall walking by the master bedroom one afternoon and getting a brief glimpse of him putting a suitcase back in his closet. Not striking me then as exceptionally odd, I did not think to mention this to my mother. After his death, as we were cleaning out his things, we opened this suitcase to find money stashed inside. What his goal was for this money is unknown to this day. Oh, the secrets this closet held.

One drawback to closets is that we fill them, so much so that when the time comes to empty them, we change our minds about the good intentions we had while filling them. Each time I have moved, I have reevaluated the need to have full closets. I typically end up donating, giving away, throwing away, or having a garage sale.

When my father died, we did all of these. When my mother died, it took me three months of donating, giving away, selling, trashing, and praying that a garage sale would relieve me of the burden that some of her "full closets" had become. I fully understand and support "saving for a rainy day," "waste not, want not," and being prepared for a possible future need. There is true value in embracing these adages. And for my mother who lived through times of want, her actions provided a measure of security, a buffer against scarcity, the benefit of options, and a feeling of control. She modeled this well for me.

Another drawback to closets is that we hang on to their contents much too long. Recently I decided to use a Velux thermal blanket that I'd kept for so long it disintegrated in my washing machine. I cleaned up thousands of tiny pieces in my washer for several weeks. Being economical and wise, keeping the blanket for sentimental reasons might be valid, but the question becomes, are our closets enhancing or detracting from our quality of life? Despite my full immersion determination to save for the future and manage my resources well, I came to realize that the things in our closets can become burdens when we hang on to them for too long. Letting go of some may be much more empowering than we expect.

Love not the world, neither the things that are in the world . . . .
And the world passeth away . . . but he that doeth the will of
God abideth forever. (1 John 2:15–17)

If you want to be perfect, go, sell what you have and give to the
poor, and you will have treasure in heaven; and come, follow
Me. (Matthew 19:21 NKJV)

SIXTEEN

AMAZING ACHIEVEMENTS

The changes in our society during my lifetime, because of the prolific technological advancements in communication, entertainment, and household machines, have been phenomenal. As an educator for nearly four decades, I had great fun demonstrating for my students the journey of some of these: from rotary telephones with expandable wall cords to smartphones; from primitive tools and utensils to household appliances such as microwaves and dishwashers; from manual typewriters to computers; from cassette tapes and boom boxes to iPods and live streaming and a mind-blowing buffet of 24/7 entertainment options. I loved watching their astonished expressions when I shared my memories of childhood some fifty years before their birth. My goal was to cultivate their background knowledge of where we have been to help them better understand how the tools available to us now did not always exist. Everything has a purpose, and each process, each advancement, leads us to the next level of growth. I wanted my students to appreciate the quality of life that these amazing achievements afford us today and be thankful. (I also simply wanted to reminisce because my memories are so powerful.)

I distinctly remember watching the funeral procession for President John F. Kennedy in November of 1963. At this time our television was still black and white as color sets were very expensive. It came with the availability of three network channels that signed off at midnight, and boasted rabbit ears. Also, you were your own remote: when you needed to adjust the antenna, change the volume, or select a new channel, you got up and turned a dial.

Most memorable for me was sitting on the family room floor in my pj's watching the first moon landing on July 20, 1969. I remember the oppressive summer heat, and we had a fan running in the window in hopes of capturing any late evening breeze. The thrill of that long-awaited moment when Neil Armstrong stepped onto the moon's surface gives me chills to this day.

We watched a lot of television when I was growing up. As one of the few readily available entertainments and a distraction from the tense silence in our house, the shows provided temporary relief from reality. My mother loved *The Ed Sullivan Show*, *The Red Skelton Show*, *The Lawrence Welk Show*, *The Carol Burnett Show*, *The Andy Williams Show*, *The Andy Griffith Show*, Mitch Miller, *The Kraft Music Hall*, and *Lassie*. I don't think a Sunday evening passed by without me crying and waving good-bye to Lassie. We also watched *My Three Sons*, *Leave It to Beaver*, *Little House on the Prairie*, *The Waltons*, *Bonanza*, *Happy Days*, *Laverne and Shirley*, *The Brady Bunch*, and *Marcus Welby, M.D.*

Perhaps because it paralleled the events occurring in the nation's space race, my favorite show was *Star Trek*. I was a

Trekkie! One of my best friends and I watched every show, memorized dialogue, bought uniform patches of the United Federation of Planets, and purchased every magazine featuring the show ever published. We even found a source to order our own personal copies of official manuscripts to read and act out.

To this day I have scrapbooks of photos of the cast and descriptions of my favorite episodes. I owned videotapes and books, many of which I still can't bear to part with. Star Trek expanded my world and led to a sense of curiosity and wonder about the possibilities of life I had never been exposed to previously. It connected me to peers on a level I had not experienced before and allowed me to have a focused outlet for creativity. It was a very personal experience in a very public domain.

Interestingly enough, the rebirth of the Star Trek phenomenon in the *Next Generation* series and movies connected me, decades later when I was a teacher, to a colleague who had also fallen in love with the show in the late '60s and early '70s. We binge watched the movies together on a regular basis. The Star Trek fascination was not short-lived for me but a recurring joyride for my imagination into the endless possibilities within God's creation.

My birth year, 1957, was the year that the Russian spacecraft Sputnik 1 initiated the space race. It was the peak of the baby boomer years, rock and roll was predominant, and *American Bandstand* began. Slinkys, hula hoops, frisbees, and the Etch A Sketch were in many kids' toy chests. Barbie would make her debut in 1959. Captain Kangaroo and Mighty Mouse had captured the attention of many. Incidentally, Dr. Seuss published *The Cat in the Hat* in 1957 as well.

The music making a social statement on the radio, both with 45 records and long play 33 1/3 records, included the big bands, of which Glenn Miller was my all-time favorite. I also loved Elvis, Ricky Nelson, Pat Boone, the Everly Brothers, Bobby Darin, and of course the Chipmunks!

The huge console stereo/radio/record player took up much of one wall in the living room of my childhood home. It was integral to the routine on Sundays, as classical instrumentals, symphonies, Beethoven, and Tchaikovsky played nearly nonstop all afternoon. Sometimes Leonard Bernstein, the Boston Philharmonic, George Gershwin, John Williams and the Boston Pops, even operatic voices such as Mario Lanza or Luciano Pavarotti, could be mixed in. One was equally likely to hear Perry Como or Bing Crosby crooning the contemporary songs of the day. My mother loved music!

We even had record players in our bedrooms. My brother, nine years my senior, had record albums for Peter, Paul and Mary, Simon and Garfunkel, the Beach Boys, the Beatles, the Doors, and Herman's Hermits. In my early collection were the Bee Gees, the Monkees, the Carpenters, the 5th Dimension, John Denver, Tony Orlando and Dawn, and Barry Manilow.

My mother's love of music did not pass me by; however, her ability to play music extended much beyond mine. She was an excellent pianist who, even as a young woman, accompanied singers in church. Her desire for me to learn to play was well meaning but unrealized as I proved not to have her talent.

The weekly music lessons she diligently took me to provided the basic skills, but I soon became painfully aware that I was far too shy to perform. Like the singer in the shower who sounds like Frank Sinatra until the water stops, I could play when I was alone but not before an audience. We had an upright piano and a small theater organ in our living room that she could make sing. I could not, to my best efforts, keep up. After about four years of lessons on both, she allowed me to stop. I am sorry she did, as making music can give such peace and joy. God's hand was in this, though, as my brother was injured in the coming months and she had to sell the piano and organ to make room for his hospital bed in the living room. Everything has a purpose.

To everything there is a season, and a time to every purpose under the heaven. (*Ecclesiastes 3:1*)

SEVENTEEN

DON'T GET YOUR HOPES UP AND YOU WON'T BE DISAPPOINTED

This has been a familiar saying in my life, established as a belief system and tradition of response. It is an effective defense mechanism against preventable emotional pain. I heard my mother say this every time something important was on the horizon.

Disappointment had probably been so crushing to her at times in her life that she developed a strategy of stoicism to deflect the potential negative emotions connected to unmet dreams. She created personal power by keeping the level of anticipation to a minimum so that if the desired outcome did not occur, the pain of letdown would also be minimized.

In theory this makes perfect sense, yet the true joys of life are not experienced fully if we do not allow ourselves to "go there" emotionally. I have used this self-protective approach and found that it is often effective at lessening my sadness when an outcome is not as I desired. I also have found that refocusing on God's will rather than my own wishes makes the outcome easier to deal with regardless of what it is.

I most recently applied this thought process to the beginning of another new school year. Each year a new class roster brings thirty or so new students into my room. Girls, boys, big, small, high achievers, average kiddos, strugglers. Some are enthusiastic learners, some are not. Some are sure this year will bring more self-esteem-crushing failures when they are not able to keep up. Others are ready to show you what they can do. Some are resentful that they must be in school and are ready to prove that they will not cooperate. Still others are just hoping that you are nice and will love them. All of them want to have fun.

Education has changed dramatically in the thirty-nine years of my career. The role of the classroom teacher has become one in which a degree in psychiatry and training in the de-escalation of intense emotional and behavioral challenges is essential. Teaching encompasses far more than basic skills instruction. Teachers often must teach basic behavioral and social skills: respect, responsibility, honesty, cooperation, problem-solving. Many children do not come to school with the basic life skills they need to function in the school setting. These are primary to being able to cultivate academic ability.

An additional challenge is the lack of support from some parents who neither value education nor want to participate actively and positively in their child's learning. They communicate to their children by word and deed that education is not important, and that teachers are making them do unnecessary work. Homework is not seen as a learning opportunity that must be taken seriously; instead, it's an inconvenience that is only done when it does not interfere with anything else. Some families live in constant crisis, so their children do not have calm, predictable, stable home lives. They come to school so needy that learning is an overwhelming challenge. They cannot sit still, maintain focus, follow directions, or complete tasks. They lose what they have done as they are so distracted or distracting to others. Teachers are powerless with little recourse in changing behavior. Parents will often complain if they do not like classroom expectations or the correction of their child. The child is always right.

Teachers are not as valued in society, not as trusted in schools, as they used to be. State standards and the barrage of required assessments have stripped teachers of the joy of teaching, the sole focus being on test scores. Teachers are micromanaged and evaluated based on student test scores. They are only viewed as successful if test scores are high. It does not matter if a student had two years of growth from where they began; if they have not achieved proficiency on the required assessed skills, they are deemed failing. So sad.

When I began my career so many decades ago, the joys of teaching were many: student relationships, those wonderful light bulb moments, seeing kiddos become lovers of learning, appreciative parents and administrators, an emphasis on knowledge and skills for a productive, happy life.

Because of the changes in education and the decline of societal support over the years, I was tempted to begin every year with the same mantra I had applied to the rest of life: "Don't get your hopes up and you won't be disappointed." But by remembering to place my trust in God to work out His plan, I began saying, "My soul, wait silently for God alone, for my expectation is from Him" (Psalm 62:5 NKJV).

EIGHTEEN

CLOSE ENCOUNTER WITH EVIL

April 19, 1995, began as any other normal day. After having driven my brother to work, I returned home to ready myself for running some errands. I gathered my purse and to-do list and headed for the door but was suddenly stopped by a strange muted "boom."

My first thought was that something in the house had malfunctioned. David's need for a wheelchair-accessible home usually led him to ranch-style construction. The drawback for me was that this house in Oklahoma had two water heaters, two furnaces, two cooling units, one of each on either side of the long, single-level floor plan. In addition, it was far enough out of the city that it used a well and a septic system. Any one of these could have been the issue.

I set out in search of the origin of the noise when I felt the ground beneath shift in what seemed like an ocean-wave rolling motion. I had felt a minor earthquake before, while in California with David, so that crossed my mind. I turned on the television hoping for some information and learned that there had been an explosion at the Alfred P. Murrah Federal Building in downtown Oklahoma City. This was about fifteen miles south of where we lived in Edmond. Needing to get on my way, and now having an idea about what the source of the unusual noise and ground movement was, I quickly got in the car and onto I-35 south. The closer I got to the city, I could see a huge plume of thick black smoke rise up on the horizon ahead.

My fellow shoppers in the grocery store were talking about what had taken place at 9:02 a.m. and the fact that the vehicle police thought was carrying the alleged bombers was thought to be headed northbound on I-35 shortly after.

Could I have driven past Timothy McVeigh and Terry Nichols on the highway? I will never know the answer to that.

After running the remainder of my errands, I arrived back home. The answering machine was blinking furiously. Cell phones were not a communication option yet, so landlines were it. My mother had left several frantic messages; fearing the worst, she had been trying to reach us, each succeeding call more desperate than the one before. I tried to call her, but for what seemed the longest time, the phone lines were full and calls were not being connected to their destinations.

When I finally reached her, she was nearly inconsolable, sobbing that she had seen the news and catastrophized to the point of believing that her children were now gone, destroyed, as she imagined the whole city to be. We spoke about what I knew of what had happened, and I assured her that all was in one piece for us.

I brought her mind back to thinking about her trip out to visit in July for our annual birthday celebrations. My birthday is in July, my father's had been in August, my brother's was in

September, and hers was in October. By the end of our talk she was calm but totally exhausted. My suspicion is that she slept for much of the remainder of the day.

The experts say that stress has many negative effects on our bodies and minds. This experience certainly did not add days to either of our lives nor fortify my level of tolerance for outrageously hurtful choices people make. PTSD is real . . . cumulative life experiences pattern our emotional responses to people, events, and circumstances, and create that expect-the-worst, straight-to-the-panic-button, zero-to-sixty, OMG, heart-stopping fear.

Over the last ten years of my teaching career, the increasing dangers of crime and violence in our society have become increasing challenges for school personnel. Schools have experienced so many more lockdowns due to police activity in surrounding neighborhoods.

A few years before I retired, a suspect being chased by the police slipped through a door just prior to its closing, trying to hide and escape through my elementary school building. We later learned that he had left the building, but in the meantime, I came face-to-face with a police officer, gun drawn, running down my hallway shouting, "Get in your room! Stay in your room!"

We rushed to be sure all students were safely in locked classrooms and spent the next hour and a half in darkened classrooms, sitting in predetermined and well-rehearsed shelter-in-place locations. Trying to keep thirty-plus students silent under these conditions for this long was miraculous. The adults in the rooms were having the same struggle, asking what was happening and how long it would go on.·

Since then many schools have become gated, locked-down,

surveillance-monitored encampments. Safety drills and disaster protocols are ever present in daily activities of teaching and learning. Dangers from the outside are compounding dangers from within as school shootings have become more common.

My last year in the classroom contributed to a pervasive sense of dread, exhaustion, and burnout. The enthusiasm I had felt over the years—excitement for each new year, new students, new opportunities—was smothered by another huge group of students, so many functioning one to three grade levels behind their peers, and some parents who did not believe in the value of education nor in supporting the work of their child and who often did not believe in the teachers. These children often knew that their parents would not support the teacher as a trusted partner, so the teacher was powerless and impotent in discipline. Pitiful!

Teachers find themselves in the roles of psychiatrist for children, counselor for parents, nutritionist and health aide, statistician for all required data proving their worth as a "highly effective" teacher to administration, the Colorado Department of Education, and the public. Insulting! Unfortunately, for some teachers it seems that students are given more benefit of the doubt than perhaps is accurate, and more influence than is reasonable in the current climate. Students and parents seem to have all the power, while teachers are evaluated and judged and labeled by the students' state-mandated test scores. No one should be held responsible for factors they cannot control: student truancy, refusal to participate, lack of parent cooperation, and often mistreatment, even bullying, of school personnel. These things are not okay! The system is broken. PTSD is becoming the norm, for evil is finding a foothold.

Where is God in all of this? He is not asleep but reminds us that free will and choice are ours to use for good or not. Believers have the knowledge and the responsibility to share truth, modeling attitudes and behaviors consistent with Scripture. Full immersion folks need to use our drive, passion, and commitment to sharing our best to demonstrate that free will and choice can be used to build relationships, support what is right, and create outcomes that are best for all. Evil does not have the ultimate power.

Therefore submit to God. Resist the devil and he will flee from you. (James 4:7 NKJV)

Be strong in the Lord and in the power of His might. Put on the whole armor of God, that you may be able to stand against the wiles of the devil. (Ephesians 6:10–11 NKJV)

Be not overcome of evil, but overcome evil with good. (Romans 12:21)

NINETEEN

ANOTHER YEAR OF SIGNIFICANT CHANGE

The moment you hold a death certificate in your hand is a moment that changes you forever. I have done this four times in my life: at the deaths of my father, my mom, my brother, and my mother-in-law. Two of these occurred within two months of each other in a year that had already held a knee-fracturing fall and the decision to complete a thirty-nine-year career in education.

My retiring was now imminent, not simply an idea any longer. I had been considering retirement from teaching for a couple years and felt that God was speaking to me clearly that 2018 would be that year. I told my fourth grade teammate, Wendy, of my plan. No surprise here as she knew my thinking about most everything. When you have a best friend in your working partner, everybody wins.

My friendship with Wendy came about late in my career. I had already taught for thirty-five years when the previous fourth grade teacher decided to retire. This left me with the opportunity to help hire the replacement who would become my new teammate. A young woman, only one year into her teaching career, applied for the position. Having met her two years earlier when she was a student teacher, I suspected she would be a great addition to our team. As I got to know her over the course of the next three years, my initial impressions were proven true. A true friendship developed despite the thirty-four-year age difference.

One day our principal observed that we enjoyed each other so much because "Wendy is an old soul, and Nancy is young at heart." For whatever reason, it worked!

I think the reason we are so close is that we care about other people's happiness. We both try to do our best to accommodate others' needs and consider relationships, not just tasks or things. Relating to people on a personal level, we both respond to situations in the same way, seeking what is best for everyone's well-being. We believe in the same values: kindness, listening, empathy, honesty, patience, humility. We both have a willingness to compromise and the ability to let others be themselves. Wendy does not compare herself to others in ways that would create stress, such as in feeling less than or competing to be better than others. I love that in her.

Our relationship was so special, however, that my talk of retirement was a substantial downer for her. Wendy had been encouraging me to tell our principal I would be retiring at the end of the school year. I looked for an opportunity to do this for several weeks, and in an impromptu meeting with just the three of us in late January, an opportunity arose. The look of astonishment on our administrator's face was one I will never forget. He just sat speechless, staring into space, as though this were the last thing he had ever imagined he would hear from me. I did not look at Wendy's face right away, knowing that her expression would be one of surprise and sadness. She was not prepared for me to make my decision public at that moment. I was correct not to look right away for her tears were flowing. Friendship, empathy, love—these things are priceless!

Through events over the next several months, God validated the appropriateness of my retirement decision as my brother became gravely ill.

David and I had gone in different directions after the death of our mother in 1999, losing touch for nearly sixteen years. It's hard to believe now that we became so disconnected. Then, in August of 2016, a strange call came to my husband's home business phone. A man neither of us knew was asking for me by my maiden name.

The man turned out to be Tony, David's friend and hired driver. Apparently David, experiencing serious health issues, had been trying to reach me for some time. He had tried writing to me, but he had an old address and his letter was returned. Eventually he asked Tony to try to find me. After a long search, he had found the phone number for Denny.

Over the next eighteen months David and I spoke frequently on birthdays, holidays, etc. I sent emails and photos to catch him up on what my life had been in the preceding years. Being as physically limited as he was, and essentially alone except for his paid health care aides, he was not able to email me, but he was able to open my emails and see the photos.

We shared memories and talked about the roads our individual lives had taken. After David and I had lost touch, he had moved from Edmond, Oklahoma, to Springfield, Missouri, and remarried. Sadly, his wife died in 2013, which left him alone once again. We talked about the challenges he was now facing. Our poignant phone conversations were fueled by the fact that we both realized his time was short.

Thankfully, Tony and his wife, Isabelle, kept me informed on David's failing health, and I felt compelled to make the long road trip to Springfield early in February.

Denny and I began the drive wondering how to manage what we might find when we arrived.

Roads on the first day were excellent; however, by the time we stopped to rest for the night, it had begun to snow. In the morning, blizzard conditions made the roadways treacherous, causing spin-offs and accidents; the remainder of the drive was harrowing. When we reached the hotel in Springfield, hours later than if the roads had been dry, we learned on the news that three people had been killed on the same road we had just been on, but we never even slid! I felt a strong sense that God had protected us during our travels, and that He had a mission for me to accomplish during our time in Springfield.

We met with Tony and Isabelle in our hotel the next afternoon and followed them to David's house. Isabelle, a retired nurse, knew what I did not: David was holding on, waiting to say good-bye to me. He needed to know that it was okay to let go.

I vividly remember Isabelle dressing me in the gown and gloves, taking me by the hand into David's room, calling out to him, "David, Nancy is here!"

I was so overwhelmed but instinctively said, "Hi, Dave. It's Nancy. I love you."

His eyes opened briefly. They were the grey-green I remembered, but dull and cloudy. I told him about the two-day drive, the bad roads, the neighbor girl watching our cats, Ginger and Dixie, so that Denny and I could come see him. His eyes were closed but I sensed that, as Isabelle said, he could hear me.

Not knowing what else to say, I chatted about my pending retirement and plans for the future. Finally, I took a deep breath and said the heart-wrenching words that, I knew now, I had come to Springfield to say.

"David, when you are ready to let go . . . it's okay to do that. Mom is waiting for you in heaven. I love you."

His eyes remained closed, but he let out a slow breath, lips pursed as though he heard, understood, and felt relief. He did not have to hold on any longer; he did not have to remain in physical pain. At this point, my inner resolve to hold myself together was drained and I got up to leave the room.

I spent the next few minutes in the hallway outside David's bedroom. Isabelle tried to offer comfort, but there was too much emotion to contain. I sobbed with an overwhelming cumulative grief for all that could have been, but also with gratitude for what had been redeemed in the past eighteen months.

Isy had known the end was very near, and that I was the person to whom David needed to say good-bye. I was the one who needed to release him so that he could let go.

David died at 6:00 a.m. the following morning.

Just thirteen hours had passed.

. . .

DENNY and I were still in the hotel room when my cell phone rang at 7:00 a.m., David's caregiver delivering the news.

What was as amazing to me as David's homegoing was Denny's reaction. My precious husband broke down in tears and said, "No more pain. David is in heaven."

Later he reminded me that God had a mission for me, that I was not going to get hurt on icy roads nor be detained from being with David to say good-bye. We'd set out for Springfield not knowing what was coming next, but God knew. He had directed us every step of the way. He knows what we need before we do (Matthew 6:8).

I was asked to write an obituary for my brother. It was my honor and privilege to do so.

But what should I say?

The unique circumstances of our lives, the sixteen years of silence, the separation of distance and experiences made this a powerful, almost burdensome task.

Through an inconceivable sequence of events, I am the only one left in our family of four.

The obituary I wrote recorded many facts:

David Walter Kent, M.D., 69 years of age, passed away in Springfield, Missouri, on Tuesday, February 6, 2018, and was welcomed into his heavenly home for eternity.

He was born on September 19, 1948, in Grand Rapids, Michigan, to mother Lorraine Nellie Newland-Kent and father Edgar Walter Kent.

After a diving accident, at age 20, left him quadriplegic, his determination and strength of character enabled him to complete his medical degree at Michigan State University.

For more than 30 years David was a Physical Medicine and Rehabilitation Specialist, practicing in Pennsylvania, Oklahoma, and Missouri. His patients were continually empowered to conquer their physical challenges through David's personal experiences, exemplary skills, and leadership.

Preceded in death by his wife, Sondra Rhone-Kent, David is survived by his sister, Nancy Kent-Koenig, and his brother-in-law, Dennis Martin Koenig.

But the words could not begin to capture the complexities of our lives. As I wrote, I remembered my sixty years of being David's sister—the struggles, emotional, spiritual, physical. I remembered lacking a father's love. I remembered a mother who tried with all of her energy to do what she thought was right. I remembered the insecurities I felt throughout so much of my life as a result of trying to be all things to all people and falling short of that so frequently. I remembered the anger I felt when David's needs superseded mine and the feeling that I had no control over my life.

I wondered if David had suspected how I'd felt, and if that had fueled the sixteen years of silence between us. I wondered if he had any idea how much his circumstances and choices had impacted and even defined my life. Perhaps he had removed himself from my life after Mom's death because he knew I could not give him more than I had already given him, which included most of my adolescence, many summers moving with him to new cities, nine years of my adulthood in Oklahoma, and three years in Michigan managing his needs from a distance.

He'd had two marriages. The first ended in divorce. The second was to Sondra, a woman with health challenges of her own, who was a caregiver for him as well as wife until her life-long struggles with fibromyalgia pain ended, on a cold December night.

David had requested that his and Sondra's ashes be laid to rest in our hometown cemetery with our parents. This required an approval from me, so I worked with the funeral home in Springfield and the cemetery in Grand Rapids to coordinate David's last wish.

David had arranged with a bank to establish a trust for him, and they had been working to complete the dispersion of his estate. I received a box containing diplomas, certificates, and photos. So many of the photos are of pieces of his life I did not recognize, whereas others I did.

I became keeper of the memories once again.

LITTLE DID Denny and I know that this loss was not to be the only one in our lives that year. Not long after returning home from saying good-bye to my brother in Springfield, I came home from working in my classroom one Sunday after-noon. As I walked in the front door, Denny met me with the news that his sister had called from Omaha to let him know that his mother, Mary, was in hospice care with cancer.

What made this all the more shocking was that, even though Mary had been ill for some time, she had kept that news from Denny.

Our next trip was to see her. We spent about a week with her talking, laughing. Denny and his brother, sister, and uncle reminisced about childhood happenings and events of their adult lives.

It is tough when these are folks you don't know very well or don't know at all. Denny's mom, dad, and sister had come to our wedding in Grand Rapids, Michigan, sixteen years before, but his brother had not attended. When Denny's father passed away, Denny had made the trip to Omaha for the funeral without me, as I was in the classroom. Now, gathering around Mary, I found myself bonding with Denny's family through our grief.

Mary amazed everyone with her strength. No prognosis could be made about how many days, or even weeks, she would be with us. I needed to be back in my classroom, having missed so many days already, so we read Scripture to her, prayed with her, told her that we knew God was with her and that, when He wanted to call her home, He would do so.

We made the long trip back home the next day. When we spoke with her on the phone, she assured us of her readiness to go to glory. Mary left us several weeks later, on April 12, 2018. Denny and I were both working. The school year would end late May, so the decision to plan a memorial service for her in early June was made.

After completing my last school year before retirement and cleaning out my classroom (now that is a monumental task after so many years!), Denny and I were on the road again. We spent time getting reacquainted with family and helping clear out Mary's house, emptying cupboards, washing windows, and cleaning carpets. My thoughts returned to my efforts in cleaning out my mother's house eighteen years before. The feelings were similar, yet also different, as these were lives I had not been engaged with for so many of the years the family had been growing. They were not deeply familiar as was my mother's home. Denny and I were given some photos and mementos to carry home to make part of our collection.

What amazed me most about the events of this year was the people God brought during our times of loss. I have Tony and Isabelle in Springfield to call friends. They were instrumental in David's life and in my experience there in February. We met a young woman working in the hotel in which we stayed who was warm and welcoming, providing us support in many ways. She connected us with her supervisor who was equally as amazing. In Omaha we found another young woman who, during each of our stays at her hotel, provided us with tangible and intangible support. Another joy was meeting Johnny, Denny's uncle. He is a kind, caring, gentle, and generous man who has a life philosophy, gleaned over his eighty-seven years, that upholds behavior consistent with Scripture. We continue to stay in touch with him long-distance.

A year of significant change? Looking back, perhaps that is an understatement. As I went into retirement, I asked myself, after all of the recent challenges, what am I ready to do? What does my back-burner passion look like?

It felt like it was time to create work that shares life experiences with others who may be facing similar crises. This past year "my cup runneth over" with people, events, places, growth in relationships, and learning more about God's faithfulness and empowerment. When He closes doors, it is time to move forward. He knows that we often won't move unless circumstances force us.

The loss of two family members and the cumulative stress

of thirty-nine years in education were clearly enough "circum-stances" for me to move on to this new endeavor in my life.

I knew that it was time to focus my full immersion mind-set in a new direction.

You will show me the path of life;
In Your presence *is* fullness of joy;
At Your right hand *are* pleasures forevermore.
(*Psalm 16:11*)

TWENTY

"BEST SELF" CONNECTIONS

Looking back, I can see that during significant changes in my life, the people who have had the biggest impact on me have been those who have demonstrated their care and support for me—the "helpers," as Mr. Rogers used to say.

Have you ever noticed that you are your "best self" around these special people, these "helpers"? They accept you and give you the sense that it is safe to be yourself around them. Realizing that perfection is not required, you feel easily, effortlessly acceptable. These true friends care enough to choose to notice the everyday aspects of who you are. They understand you when you are quiet; they listen and reflect when you share.

A few times in my life I have met people (or I should say, God brought people into my life) who are genuinely caring human beings who bring out my desire to be my best self. The blessing of encouragers in unexpected places is the embodiment of 1 Thessalonians 5:11: "Encourage one another and build each other up" (NIV).

One of the most special people is Wendy, my young teacher teammate. She is one of the kindest, most caring young women I have ever known. Her life has not been without its struggles, but her desire to do what is right guides her actions toward her mother, dad, husband, and job. She is stronger than she realizes. Our relationship filled my need for the sister and daughter I never had, and the best friend I really wanted. Her focus is on positivity, and she chooses to notice the good first. She became even more a treasure to me as Denny and I walked through the deaths of both my brother and his mother.

Two other colleagues, Elizabeth and Tina, have had their own challenges with family and personal health yet my friendships with them have been an immeasurable blessing to me.

Then there is George, a gentleman I have known for over a decade. A classroom teacher at heart, George later became a social worker and administrator. George knows what it takes to be successful. He sees students through the lens of an experienced educator and uses life lessons to guide interactions; he knows that using natural consequences for choices creates powerful teachable moments. I was so grateful for his support of both me and my students. His realistic, pragmatic, common-sense approach to building relationships is refreshing.

God can bring beauty to all seasons of our lives. We may not relish every season—some are quite painful—yet He provides us with strength through the people He brings across our path. Folks like Nellie, a beautiful senior who is still working full-time at age seventy-eight, outworking everyone around her. Nellie came into my life during the trips that Denny and I made to Omaha, Nebraska, to be with Mary, Denny's mom. Nellie works in a restaurant in Kearney, Nebraska. She immediately bonded with us as conversation revealed our Christian values. She treated us like family each time we stopped in to eat and rest from our drive. She demonstrated her strength of character and her faith in how she treated the other workers in the restaurant as well as her customers. Everyone loved and respected her. Her faith was so openly evident, strong and determined, even when facing the loss of her husband to cancer. People are drawn to her because of her warmth, gentleness, and trust in God. She loves unconditionally.

Another senior, Denny's uncle, Johnny, is eighty-seven and still going strong. He worked diligently for many decades to build a life for his family. He and his wife, Beverly, were married for sixty years. The last several were extremely difficult as Beverly fought and lost her battle with Alzheimer's. Having to relinquish her too soon was heartbreaking and came not too many years before losing his sister (Denny's mom) to cancer. The days we spent together during our visits to Omaha, sitting in the hospice care facility talking, navigating the overwhelming emotions of the funeral, and moving on with life less one loving person, all demonstrated the amazing qualities he possesses but feels too shy to share openly.

I was honored to have some one-on-one time with Johnny. He told me how lonely and sad he was being without his wife, and now his sister, and how shy he felt. He wanted to reach out to others but "chickened out" every time he had an opportunity to interact. He said he admired how I try new things, adding wistfully, "You have a good brain to figure things out."

I think we connected so deeply because I am the last of my family—a survivor—and so is he. I am the keeper of the family memories—so is he. We both have insecurities that have influenced decisions we've made, yet God brought us together to make a difference in each other's lives.

Eleanor Roosevelt believed that "many people will walk in and out of your life, but only true friends will leave footprints in your heart."

And I couldn't agree more. Trust among friends brings joy and empowers us each to be our best self, the self God created us to be. I am so grateful that, though I have given Christ countless reasons not to love me, none of them changed His mind. He continues to amaze me with His grace.

My grace is sufficient for you, for my power is made perfect in weakness. (2 Corinthians 12:9 NIV)

TWENTY-ONE

JEALOUSY

Jealousy in my life leads me to think and do things that are inconsistent with the person I strive to be.

Comparing myself to others and feeling like I don't measure up creates a sense of anger in me.

I try to refocus, reframe my thinking with gratitude: *I am a child of God and His creation.* Colossians 3:23 reminds us, "And whatsoever ye do, do it heartily, as to the Lord, and not unto men." I know that thoughts have energy and my attitude can change my circumstances.

Charles R. Swindoll said, "Life is 10% what happens to you and 90% how you react to it." Theodore Roosevelt said, "Believe you can and you're halfway there." Small steps in the right direction can turn out to be the biggest steps of your life.

My full immersion personality pushes me to do more and do it better, and sometimes that contributes to jealousy. What comes easy won't last long, and what lasts long won't come easy.

Growing up as a short, overweight, painfully shy young

person, often teased and bullied about my body, I continued to feel like an outsider in most every social encounter. Even as an adult, I felt defeated, hurt, embarrassed, and angry at the world for not recognizing the person I was inside.

Struggling with these kinds of self-doubt and insecurities, my full immersion focus and intensity spurred me to chase perfection, making me quick to take the blame and apologize for less than perfect results, whether I needed to or not. I became a human "doing" rather than a human "being." This was consistent with the expectations of my mother who had been raised with a Puritan work ethic that says your value comes from your accomplishments.

I always felt "less than," like I did not measure up, so I would strive to be good enough, to please, while constantly filled with self-doubt.

And I am not alone.

Recently a colleague shared with me that she was having trouble with jealousy. Her confession surprised me, as she appears to be the epitome of control in so many areas of her life —time management, personal organization, classroom management—and doing all these things with great success.

And yet here she was, telling me that she was miserable and angry, convinced that acknowledgment that was due to her had gone to someone else instead.

Theodore Roosevelt aptly stated, "Comparison is the thief of joy," and I saw in my colleague this very struggle.

Education is a multidimensional performing art. Teachers work so diligently to gain the results we are required to achieve, and a preoccupation with accountability creates a sense of failure and blame. A pervasive dark cloud of angst surrounds us as we are continuously observed, evaluated, and critiqued, even though many of the factors influencing student learning—factors like class size, truancy, lack of home support, deficiency in prior knowledge, basic skills, and self-control—are out of our control.

Today's angst-ridden environment of the teaching profession, often filled with a sense of failure and blame, breeds resentfulness, competition, and jealousy. So much pressure to "do more" only serves to increase the frustration, when so much already being done does not change kids who refuse to cooperate or give consistent effort. Teachers are trying to make a difference in a broken system.

The experience of my colleague was a wake-up call of sorts for me. I realized that my personal focus needed to change so that I did not continue to experience the heart-wrenching frustration and physical, emotional exhaustion I'd lived with most of my life.

I needed to find a way to worry less about what others seem to have that I do not.

I remind myself often of the words of Eleanor Roosevelt: "No one can make you feel inferior without your consent."

What an empowering concept!

When I feel "less than" or judged, I ask myself who has walked in my shoes? Who knows me so well as to give an accurate judgment?

Mrs. Roosevelt also stated, "You wouldn't worry so much about what others think of you if you realized how seldom they do." So true! Some people thrive on what others think and end up becoming different than who they really are. Stay true to yourself and what you believe God wants for you. No one is you, and that is your superpower.

I love the saying that goes, "What is for you will not pass

you." What a huge blessing it is to know and rest in this. We can't really know what others are experiencing, what burdens they carry, or what kind of pain they have experienced that causes them to behave as they do. Jealousy destroys quality of life if we allow it to. Hanging on to feelings of anger and jealousy exhausts the body, brain, and soul. God wants us to consider what is important: "Set your affection on things above, not on things on the earth" (Colossians 3:2). The Bible also tells us, "Lay up for yourselves treasures in heaven . . . For where your treasure is, there will your heart be also" (Matthew 6:20–21).

I am realizing that my childhood insecurities—the source of so much struggle for so many years—do not need to define me. I am who I am today because of influences I could not control, choices I made along the way, and the opportunities God has brought into my life.

Today is His gift to each of us, and living it well, as God has instructed, brings happiness. This is how we live above the trouble that "having trouble with jealousy" can bring.

Let your conversation be without covetousness; and be content with such things as ye have: for he hath said, I will never leave thee, nor forsake thee. (Hebrews 13:5)

TWENTY-TWO

BEING PART OF SOMEONE ELSE'S MIRACLE

I once was told by a friend, "One day someone is going to hug you so tight that all your broken pieces will stick back together." Thankfully, I've been blessed to have a few of these folks enter my life at strategic times. All were miracles, exemplifying the love of God in their words and actions, and "paying it forward" in ways that none of them realized they were doing.

Galatians 6 focuses on doing good to all and bearing one another's burdens. What a special joy it is to have a part in God's plan in someone else's journey. God has allowed me to be part of other people's lives in this way also, simply because I cared for them enough to pay attention. Miracles aren't necessarily shouts; often they are whispers.

And sometimes we don't know what impact we have had on others until our time together is drawing to a close and we are about to go our separate ways.

My years in education reaffirmed this many times. Many special students, parents, and colleagues have left their imprint on my heart, creating powerful, life-altering experiences and memories. So many of these "whispers" might have easily gone unnoticed.

One such special student was Wesley. Wes was an eighth grader who came for academic support to my special education resource room at NorthPointe Middle and High School. His mom and dad had adopted him years before and, wanting the best supportive learning environment for him, decided to send him to a Christian school. They provided him everything they could, the best opportunities to grow up strong and happy. He was their miracle child.

Unfortunately, Wes became fascinated by a dangerous hanging "game" he learned about from older students. He had no real understanding of the seriousness of his actions. The outcome for Wes was devastating. At the memorial service, his dad shared that I had been a blessing to their family. He shared that Wes had loved me for his teacher and felt that I truly loved him. He appreciated the help I had provided his son, but more so the daily words of support and encouragement to keep on learning and becoming his best self. Proverbs 25:11 tells us, "A word fitly spoken is like apples of gold in pictures of silver." We many never know the impact our words or example mean to others, but sometimes circumstances allow us this knowledge.

Another miracle kiddo who blessed my life was Lynn. This youngster was so talented, she was advanced to fourth grade even though she was a second grader by age. Her mom, also a teacher, recognized the challenges she was having in adapting to being unique. The socio-emotional needs of gifted children present as many, if not more, challenges than their academic ones. My goal became letting Lynn lead her learning, keeping her challenged in learning something that she did not already know every day. She became our expert, once a week teaching her classmates what she had been learning. In this way she grew in her skills, self-confidence, and ability to communicate her knowledge with her peers. Through tears of joy at the end of the school year, Mom shared her gratitude that Lynn had flourished in my classroom. She had grown academically, but more importantly, she had found her voice and the joy of being who she was. This was indeed a sweet miracle.

So many families are struggling to manage the responsibilities of life and cannot meet all the needs young children have in trying to find their way. A young lady who made a lasting memory for me was Jaime. When we first met, she was angry and not accepting of others, acting out toward them in problematic ways. I was fairly certain that her needs for security and respect were not being met at home. I spent time building a relationship with her in hopes of gaining trust so critical for any learning to take place. Gradually she began to accept help, and a wonderful bond was created. Building self-acceptance, confidence, and trust freed up the passion she had for learning. By the end of the school year, she had not only gained the competencies she needed to catch up with her peers but exceeded the expectations for mastery of grade-level content. I have kept the beautiful thank-you letter, attached to an extra-large teddy bear, that she gave me at the end of the year. Miracles happen when we are willing to do our part in someone else's life.

One of the most cherished events for teachers is to be requested by a parent whose other children you have worked with before. The relationship you've built with an older child leads to the parent's desire to trust you to nurture a younger sibling, which is significant for a teacher.

The most memorable of these events for me involved the children of two families, the Robbs and the Gregs. Both were juggling the challenges of multigenerational caregiving in daily family life. The oldest Robb child, Craig, seemed overwhelmed by the demands of his roles at home and school.

I vividly recall begging Craig's mother to help me help him in the first conference I could get her to attend. I believe that it was because of my refusal to accept failure in Craig's life that he finally put an effort into his own learning. Perhaps Mom was finally convinced by my passionate pleas for her participation that she actively engaged in her son's development. He returned to visit with me on many occasions to share successes, and with the anticipation that I would encourage him to continue giving his best efforts. His little brother, Chris, was even more reluctant to do the work, even though accomplishment came easier for him than for his older brother. To see the change in Mom's participation in her children's education, from distant and frozen in helplessness to engaged and supportive, and the successes gained as a result is truly miraculous! Craig Robb is now a successful high school student who is determined to complete his education.

In similar fashion, the Greg boys stand out in my mind as miracle kiddos. Large families like theirs often face challenges trying to accommodate everyone's needs. This was certainly true for Sam and Paul. Learning tasks presented few hurdles for Sam, and as the oldest son he had more of Dad's attention than Paul did. Paul felt this difference acutely, and his willingness to try was obviously impacted. He believed that he did not matter.

When I met him, the family was separated by many miles as Mom had taken a job with a commute too substantial to make more than every few weeks. Dad was managing the home as a single parent, focusing on the big issues, which did not leave him much time or energy for little Paul. I made it my mission to fill in some of the emotional support for him. By the end of the year, Paul had successfully achieved the goals we needed him to reach, and even surpassed expectations by not only participating in the school-wide science fair but winning his category, which qualified him to attend the district science competition. Amid lots of splendid entries, he placed in his category. Miraculous, absolutely!

I have enjoyed students who were super capable and simply needed instruction, others who found academic experiences somewhat daunting, and some who came to school already having surrendered long ago to failure as a way of life. Anna, Ellie, and Carl were a teacher's dream students—high-achieving, perceptive learners who simply needed to develop a few additional basic skills in order to soar. Mark and Andy found learning a bit challenging until passions were identified and integrated into classroom work. Mark found energy in partnering with other students, Andy in plays and theater, where becoming another character freed him to shine personally. Mariah had experienced so much defeat in her learning experiences that she used avoidance to keep from facing yet another self-esteem-crushing failure. My miracle kiddo found her voice through social studies and shone like a star in her presentation of her historic character in our "Night of the Notables" wax museum program. I will never forget her walking enthusiastically around and around our classroom practicing her "famous person" speech. From fragile and defeated to strong and empowered—a truly miraculous transformation!

My last year in the classroom was the most memorable to me for some obvious reasons, but also for some less discernible ones. Over the course of my career, I have met some young people who changed me as a person. Jason was one of those kids. He was shuttled back and forth between his parents' and grandparents' homes, as his very young parents were in and out of jail on drug charges. His grandmother, whom I grew to love and respect, was still working full-time, caring for her husband, who had experienced trauma in the military, and working with counselors and later the court system to adopt Jason and his younger sister. Jason faced challenges that created some emotional and psychological disabilities for him. He demonstrated some passive-aggressive anger issues, anxiety, and depression. At times he really wanted to please and was sorry for his behavior. At other times he would argue and be defiant such that I would just let him be. He spent time with the school social worker, went to counseling every week, and knew that it was okay to sit alone in the back of the classroom if that was what he needed to do. At first he pulled away from much interaction, but as the weeks and months went by, he was trusting enough to reach out to me for encouragement, support, and even hugs. This was a miracle. Each little step forward, though threatened by occasional steps backward, was a miracle, a light in a great deal of darkness for Jason.

I fully believe that God knows what each of us needs and brings people into our lives at the most meaningful times. Sometimes we need, or need to provide, a word of acceptance or encouragement; sometimes a smile that communicates "I understand you." Perhaps we may need, or need to share, a reassuring touch or a hug. So much can be communicated with these small gestures. Being there for someone else can be as special as having someone meet your need. Miracles are available for each of us to be part of if we care enough to pay attention. We never want to miss an opportunity to experience a miracle . . . even if it's just a whisper.

My mouth shall speak of wisdom; and the meditation of my heart shall be of understanding. (Psalm 49:3)

Train up a child in the way he should go, and when he is old he will not depart from it. (Proverbs 22:6 NKJV)

TWENTY-THREE

BOUNDARIES

I have never been super confident with relationships as I'm always uncertain of the "rules." My personal needs and space have so frequently been compromised by others for their needs that I am always questioning what is appropriate:

How should I respond?

Is it okay to say no or have a differing opinion?

What are the boundaries?

Throughout my life—with my mother and father's volatile relationship; my brother's injury and the resulting new dynamic of stress; my father's death; my mother's health decline, move to Oklahoma, and subsequent loss to Alzheimer's and dementia—relationship boundaries were never consistently clear. After my return to Grand Rapids to bury her and then my move back there, trying to help David still in Oklahoma, getting married, completing my second graduate school program, reestablishing my career, moving to Colorado—somehow these all kept me focused on tasks, rather than relationships, for decades. Throughout my life I immersed myself in the requirements of each of these responsibilities—the completion of the tasks involved—more so than the connection to the people in these relationships. It was less painful this way. I did not have to struggle as intensely with my own questions and self-doubt. I would just do. And I never found satisfactory answers to these powerful questions.

Marrying Denny meant figuring out a whole new level of "rules" as we established our marriage partnership and navigated space, responsibilities, finances—and the surprises these discoveries often uncover. Blending two middle-aged people's individual experiences, hurts, frustrations, needs, and hopes into one life is a true adventure. Big issues present some challenges, yet some of the seemingly insignificant details are equally important: Which side of the bed? What groceries? What routines for household chores? What should be holiday traditions and expectations?

Each time a major change took place in my life, the familiar question "What do people want from me?" popped up. When I returned to Grand Rapids to bury my mom and clean out her condo, I was searching for myself, so excited about the possibilities now that I had some freedom. What was I going to do, a forty-three-year-old woman who had never really had a normal adolescence?

I found myself in my hometown but not at home in the true sense. I needed to determine what to do not only with Mom's stuff but also with my new life.

Curiously, I found myself fending off unwanted relationships and trying to understand what a healthy relationship looked like in this new frontier. Not an easy task sometimes. I saw personal evidence that unless we live by what we know to be God's truth, and God's boundaries, the world will consume us.

Working in food service for a bit to decide if I wanted to continue teaching or forge a new career, I met some of the most unique characters—people making life and moral choices I would never have made myself. Many of these people did not share my values. Others were simply trying to survive and were clueless on how to interact with others in a healthy, respectful manner.

Fortunately, I was not naïve as some thought I might be, and I managed to weed out the players from those wanting to be authentic. There were definitely more players than I had experienced before! Being raised as I was and working in Christian school environments much of my career, this was quite eye-opening. I learned a lot about how hard the world can be and how cautious one must be to guard against the users. I learned that I could be strong, independent, and self-sufficient rather than simply a provider for a needy family. I saw evidence of God's purpose for everything, His preparation for the next steps I was to make.

Even in hindsight today, I do not fully understand all that I have experienced in my life. But I know that these things are true:

- I must persevere to allow God's work in me to continue:

God has begun a good work in me and will perform it until the day of Jesus Christ. (Philippians 1:6)

I must not be weary in doing good. (Galatians 6:9)

God's works will endure forever. (Ecclesiastes 3:14)

- I need not be perfect:

His way is perfect. (Psalm 18:30)

The Lord will perfect whatever concerns me. (Psalm 138:8)

His grace is sufficient, and His strength is made perfect in weakness. (2 Corinthians 12:9)

PERHAPS I WILL ALWAYS WONDER about boundaries, always wonder what is right and good in my relationships with the world. I have learned many lessons in my six decades of life, some pertaining to money, position, and career, and some to interpersonal connections and spirituality. I know that being a people pleaser, comparing myself to others, taking everything too personally, and trying to control everything leads to sadness, frustration, and regret. Not a fulfilling life!

Despite my birth family, my caregiving responsibilities, my fears and insecurities, my struggle with weight and small stature, I can see that every day God sustains me and helps me pursue my best life. He continues to show me what it means to be full immersion with its most positive qualities. He continues to nurture the "me" He created and loves—the "me" I need to accept. I am worthy to create my own boundaries and be myself.

God is not finished revealing the story He is writing for my life.

And He's not finished in your life either.

> *Delight thyself also in the* LORD, *and he shall give thee the desires of thine heart.* (Psalm 37:4)

TWENTY-FOUR

WHAT'S IN A NAME?

I've always been amazed by the reactions people have to their names. Children are super attentive to names, their own and those of others. The beginning of every school year brought the somewhat daunting task of matching thirty or more new students' names with faces. I invariably gave the disclaimer and request that I had so many new names to learn and my students just had one, mine, so they needed to be patient and respectful with me as I mastered who was who.

The task was often made more challenging by the number of siblings of previous years' students who looked very similar, the uniqueness of some names, the preponderance of names beginning with the same letter (e.g., Jasmine, Jayden, Jason, and Jackson), and students who simply reminded me former students.

Some kiddos preferred a nickname or had been in the same classroom throughout their school years with another child of the same name, so a nickname minimized identity confusion and basically preserved sanity, mine in particular.

What never failed to happen was the reaction if a mistake was made in applying a name incorrectly. Voices were raised, some coming to the defense of the child for which the misnomer was used, some eager just to prove the teacher wrong. In any case, a chorus of chastising name redirection occurred.

I truly do understand this. Names are very personal, and we react to hearing our own, even if it was actually intended for someone else. Names have meaning (for example, Nancy means grace). Names also bring back memories, whether satisfying or disturbing.

Growing up in the 1960s, before computers, cell phones, and the multitude of streaming and gaming devices, children played outside. We would be out until the streetlights came on or until we heard our names called from front porches or open windows. Our group would continuously downsize as kids disappeared to the sound of their names being broadcast.

My mother would stand on the front porch and loudly call out. If she had to walk to the corner, look down the street, and call again, the tone changed. If she called more than a few times, usually a reprimand was at hand. I could tell by the tone with which she called "Nancy!" roughly the mood she was in at that point.

In the six decades of my life there have been a few people whose use of my name has made me smile. Once such person was my brother who often called me Nancer. Another was a colleague who always yelled her greeting, "Hey, Nanc!" even if she was within ten feet of me. My husband has a certain cadence, a rhythm, when he calls to me from another room, but the most unique sound of my name has just recently come into my world. My brother-in-law, Gary, who literally shouts my name rapid-fire, as though the two syllables are compressed into one. His pronunciation is as intense as his personality.

What is more personal than a gift with your name monogrammed, imprinted, or stitched? Or having someone autograph a book or piece of art to you with your name? We are especially moved when we are able to touch the name of a lost soul at a war memorial or cemetery.

What a sweet blessing to know that God calls us by name as His children, and we have the privilege of calling on Him by name . . . now that's a true gift of eternal value!

Because he hath set his love upon me, therefore will I deliver him; I will set him on high, because he hath known my name.
(Psalm 91:14)

TWENTY-FIVE

CALLING BACK MY SPIRIT

What is my purpose in life?

Am I thriving or just surviving?

What makes my heart sing?

If I had one year to live, how might I live it?

Societal expectations put pressure on us to behave in a way that may not be the essence of our true selves. We become trapped by the need to keep juggling the responsibilities we have. We become emotionally exhausted, physically depleted, and sometimes ill—emotionally, physically, mentally, or spiritually. Overloaded, overwhelmed, powerless, we can spiral down to burnout.

I certainly was there.

For decades I worked to care for family, students, parents, and colleagues, and tried to create and support a lifestyle I rarely really got to enjoy.

For many people challenges become stressors as the number of responsibilities increases. Too many demands become stress, then frustration, sometimes anger, and then withdrawal. We begin to feel that we cannot do all that is expected of us. Our self-esteem can drop.

That was me as well. Teaching was my job, but it became my identity. I no longer had the energy left for cultivating "self." I lost sight of my purpose, my spirit, my connection with me. I certainly was not thriving . . . only barely surviving.

In searching for help to keep moving forward, I learned that our early experiences can be biologically embedded in our brains and bodies and can have long-lasting effects on our behavior. A negative childhood environment can affect our health and behavior for decades to come, if we let it. Our thoughts and words are alive; they have energy and power. Thankfully, we can reframe the negative to become positive affirmations. Changing our thoughts can change our lives. We have the spiritual resources in Christ to overcome all these challenges.

Philippians 3:12–14 reminds us to forget what is behind and reach for what is ahead with joy.

Philippians 4:8–9 encourages us to think on those things that have virtue.

Psalm 51:12 states that if we ask, God will restore the joy of our salvation and uphold us with a willing spirit.

Colossians 3:13 states that we must forgive as Christ forgave to have true freedom to move ahead, and verses 15 through 17 emphasize the importance of thankfulness.

My life's work has been education, and as a lifelong learner I believe that knowledge is power. Gratitude is also empowering, as it makes a world of difference if you can be thankful that you have a cup, not just that it is half full.

You know what else is empowering? Forgiveness. Forgiveness is about taking back our power. When we forgive, we are no longer a victim in the story of our life. We are in control of how we feel. Forgiveness is about healing ourselves, not about healing or helping the people who hurt us or let us down. It empowers us to let go of the past and walk forward with God into beautiful new places of grace. We are children of God, a spark of the Divine. Everything happens for a reason, and we each hold the key to transform our lives by acting on these foundational principles.

Our spirituality makes us more resilient, hopeful, content, and at peace with ourselves and our lives. Belief in God is the greatest stress reducer.

As I now move from nearly four decades in education into the years of my life in which I do not have the constraints of a full-time job, I am asking myself, *What does personal success look like, feel like, now? What calls back my spirit and makes my heart sing? What is God asking me to do?*

The image of God closing and opening doors for His children is intriguing to me. When I have approached a crossroads, perhaps a defining moment in my life, I have envisioned a doorway. My choice is to stand there holding the doorknob tightly going nowhere or try to open it to see what would happen. When I focus on the good I might discover by being willing to walk through, the outcomes frequently amaze me. Seems profoundly simple, doesn't it?

In the popular song "Live Like You Were Dying," country music legend Tim McGraw asks us to consider how we will respond to life's tragedies. Possible responses include rethinking priorities, admitting mistakes, and making some changes. He encourages us to live as though tomorrow is a gift and to think about what to do with it. Considering this carefully, we should live as if we were dying.

A dear friend of mine recently received a cancer diagnosis. What do you do when this happens to you? I imagine that you begin to rethink your priorities, perhaps make some changes, and do things that make your heart sing. My friend is doing all of these. She has been considering medical options of course, but she has also begun to reevaluate what means the most to her now.

I often ask myself, if I had one year or less to live, how might I live it? What a powerful motivation to choose purposefully. How do I want to spend my time? What makes my heart sing? For me the answer now is writing—the creative, heartfelt expression of acceptance, validation, appreciation, and thankfulness. And living fully immersed of course, as I don't know another way. This is who God created me to be.

What makes *your* heart sing?

See then that ye walk circumspectly, not as fools, but as wise, redeeming the time, because the days are evil. Wherefore be ye not unwise, but understanding what the will of the Lord is.
(Ephesians 5:15–17)

TWENTY-SIX

BROWNIES

"Don't let your job define your happiness" is a saying I have heard before but never applied to my life prior to the last few years of my career. Teaching was my life, my passion, my hobby, my identity. I thought about my students more than their parents did in some cases, and I continuously worked to improve my instruction. I began to see many of my colleagues increasingly frustrated, overworked, and exhausted. Most of us were feeling underappreciated in our school and devalued by parents and society as a whole. I could see burnout imminent for several of my teammates.

Joyce Meyers states, "Happiness is not a feeling, it is a choice. To be happy, one must choose to be happy, not respond to a circumstance that now controls your happiness."

Before I retired, I tried an experiment. Hoping that I might bring encouragement to others, if only briefly, I began doing something that I love, which is baking (remember the zucchini bread?). In particular, I began baking brownies. I started bringing brownies to special events, especially for birthdays and Friday treats. This escalated into movie nights, bake sales, classroom achievement celebrations, etc. I honored requests but sometimes would simply show up with a little foil-wrapped package for someone having more struggles than usual.

This little treat was enough to make a smile appear every time. What a sweet surprise to walk into your classroom or office and find a small silver packet waiting for you! Smiles of recognition would greet me as I walked through the building with these treats, and I developed a following—literally, a following. Eyes would follow me down the hallway until I was out of sight and the realization settled in that the treat was for someone else. I was told that I had become famous for my brownies. One of my administrators said, "I am a happy man," as he realized he had been the recipient of the coveted silver packet. Students called me the "brownie teacher," requesting to be in my classroom when they reached fourth grade. I was told that a parent, at a movie night, once offered five dollars for the brownies that remained on a plate on the dessert table!

This simple idea took on a life of its own, and I have received more smiles, hugs, and tears of joy over little silver packages than I can count. One person can make a difference —one little silver brownie packet at a time! Everybody needs a cheering section.

The first Christmas after I had retired, I showed up at the school to deliver multiple pans of deliciousness to the teachers' lunchroom. You never know the impact you've had on others until you are not there any longer and suddenly pop in for a visit. To see my colleagues struggling with exhaustion, work overload, and frustration with too many needy students was difficult, yet providing them with a treat, words of encouragement, and hugs hopefully made the day a bit easier.

My former students, now fifth graders, were gone on a field trip, so I did not get to see them—and I smiled to myself that now I had a good reason to make a return visit. It seemed odd to walk down hallways that were still so familiar to me, to peek into the classroom that had been mine for twelve years, and to see it rearranged and filled with another teacher's things. Remembering the struggle of trying to meet the needs of all my students and all the requirements of assessments, I was flooded with gratitude that I did these things to the best of my ability and ministered to the kiddos as if they were my own, but that those days were in the past.

Was it worth it? Yes. Did I make a difference? Yes.

My purpose in returning was to share friendship, inspiration, and little silver packets of brownie happiness!

Was it worth it? Yes. Did I make a difference? Yes.

Do to others as you would have them do to you. (Luke 6:31 NIV)

TWENTY-SEVEN

MR. ROGERS AND NEW BEGINNINGS

The older I get, and the more I reflect about the life experiences I've had thus far, the more appreciative I am of the simple yet profound lessons of Fred Rogers, star of *Mister Rogers' Neighborhood*. His model of kind and compassionate acceptance of all people is so essential to living as Christ demonstrated.

He realized that people need to know they are acceptable. We are all unique and valuable, and we all make a difference in other people's lives simply because we are alive. Mr. Rogers said, "If you could only sense how important you are to the lives of those you meet; how important you can be to the people you may never even dream of. There is something of yourself that you leave at every meeting with another person." As an educator, I know my influence often extended beyond what I realized at the time.

Mother Teresa believed, "I cannot change the world, but I can cast a stone across the waters to create many ripples." She said, "Let no one ever come to you without leaving better and happier. Be the living expression of God's kindness."

I believe that no learning and no kindness is ever wasted. Kindness makes people feel good about themselves, inspires them to be their best. I knew that my students would forget much of what we did during our year together, but they would remember how I made them feel. The connections we make in our lifetimes—the encouraging, validating words we speak—are so important. They may be what heaven is like! In the words of Mr. Rogers, "In the external scheme of things, shining moments are as brief as the twinkling of an eye, yet such twinklings are what eternity is made of—moments when we human beings can say 'I love you,' 'I'm proud of you,' 'I forgive you,' 'I'm grateful for you.' That's what eternity is made of: invisible imperishable good stuff."[1]

I've always believed what Scripture says about a time and a purpose for everything. God knows the why and the how, where I am now, and longs to influence my choices impacting the future. We all are works in progress, and God leads by closing doors and opening windows. In education we speak of a necessary "growth mind-set." In life it is essential to have a Christ mind-set, seeing through His lens.

I could never have imagined the events God would use to influence my mind-set. The death of two family members within two months of each other served to intervene and change my life focus. I love this Mr. Roger's quote: "Often when you think you're at the end of something, you're at the beginning of something else." The end of something was clear, but the beginning of "something else" was not.

Pain is part of life, and working through challenges can

cause us to grow. God asked me to end the career that had been my life's work and identity for nearly four decades. Transitions are difficult for me. I feel out of control and have a sense of loss even though I know to grow I have to leave things behind. I have to create a new normal.

In *The Problem of Pain,* C. S. Lewis wrote, "Pain insists upon being attended to. God whispers to us in our pleasure, speaks to us in our consciences, but shouts in our pain. It is a megaphone to rouse a deaf world."[2]

As I read this, my ever-present arthritis pain cried out for my attention and my thoughts turned to prayer: *Oh God, what am I missing. What do you want to show me? I am listening.*

There have been many occasions in my life when God has used physical pain to grab my attention: a broken foot, a fractured patella (twice), DVT (deep vein thrombosis) blood clots in my left leg, shingles, sciatica, an arthritis-generated bone spur in my knee, tendinitis in my wrist.

Each time my pain—and the inevitable downtime that came with it—served to turn my focus to God. Pain drives us to find solutions. Crying out for help and making an action plan to regain strength allowed me time to reflect, realign priorities, and wait on Him to show me the next step. James 1:2–4 reminds us that trials make us strong.

I believe that to hurt is to know, to fail is to grow, and to lose is to gain because most of life's greatest lessons are learned through pain—physical, emotional, psychological, and spiritual. God uses our deepest pain as the launching pad of our greatest calling. Pain invites us to acknowledge our weakness and vulnerability, and to make time to realign priorities, refocus, and renew our purpose.

The last year of my teaching career was the perfect storm of pain, consisting of months of exhaustion from dragging around the knee brace supporting a fractured patella, the death of two family members, and God's voice telling me thirty-nine years in education was enough. He had another plan for me: retirement and new creative opportunities.

No one is perfect. Consider the encouragement provided by the characters of the Bible who were clearly not perfect but used of God anyway. I'm sure they felt as if they were in impossible predicaments, as we often do today.

Some days even our best efforts fall short of what we would like to be able to do, but doing what we can with what we have is the most we should expect of ourselves and anyone else. A willingness to keep trying matters most.

Disappointment, guilt, anger, and pride can all be forces leading to creative achievement and potentially to dreams coming true. We must be realistic and recognize that some wishes will never come true and be willing to put the energy they consumed into those things we *can* do.

Discovering the truth about ourselves is a lifetime's work, but it's worth the effort. Who we are in the present includes who we were in the past. Since we rarely have time for everything we want in this life, choices must be made. My choices now include using my past to make me better rather than bitter and focusing on who I am in Christ. God sees us as worthy, imperfections included!

Joyce Meyers instructs us to "strive for excellence, not perfection, because we don't live in a perfect world."

One of my favorite poems is "Stopping by Woods on a Snowy Evening" by Robert Frost. While appreciating beauty and solitude during a winter's evening carriage ride through the woods, the author is reminded that he has "promises to keep" and "miles to go before I sleep."

We all have promises to keep and miles yet to journey, and it is up to us to seek God's desires for our next direction. We are better prepared when we take time to stop, listen, and be in the moment. Where will your miles take you? How will you use the rest of the miles you are given? Our prayers should be for wisdom and joy, and that in every ending we will see new beginnings.

We will make space for celebration of what has been achieved.

Not everyone has the same capabilities for wealth, health, beauty, etc., but all of us can decide when something is enough. There is no such thing as not good enough; however, there is such a thing as not the right time. We can devote our full immersion energies to forgiving, loving, nurturing, encouraging, and inspiring others and ourselves.

And perfection is never required.

That's the "good stuff."

The LORD is my shepherd; I shall not want.
He maketh me to lie down in green pastures: he leadeth me
beside the still waters.
He restoreth my soul: he leadeth me in the paths of
righteousness for his name's sake.
Yea, though I walk through the valley of the shadow of death, I
will fear no evil: for thou art with me; thy rod and thy staff they
comfort me.

Thou preparest a table before me in the presence of mine enemies: thou anointest my head with oil; my cup runneth over. Surely goodness and mercy shall follow me all the days of my life: and I will dwell in the house of the LORD *forever.*

(*Psalm* 23)

TWENTY-EIGHT

NO REGRETS

Each of us has made decisions that we thought were best. As can happen, we often look back and reevaluate the motivations for making the choices we did. Sometimes the outcome was not what we anticipated because we did not have enough information to make a different choice. As can also happen, our decisions can be misunderstood, and we experience the negative responses this can bring. It is often said that perception is reality and no one can really know the life experiences of another person that cause them to interpret reality in their own unique way. Sometimes they are fearful or insecure, and you become the unsuspecting casualty in their attempts to feel better about themselves.

As Mother Teresa once said, "Sometimes people come into your life as blessings. Some come into your life as lessons."

I thought that I was a fairly decent judge of character and had a good grasp on reading people's behavior, but I found a whole new social order when I moved from Christian to public education. I had students steal from me and lie to me and others. This I could deal with, but when I realized that adults were also doing these things—taking ideas and work they had not created for their own—I questioned my decision to become part of this environment.

Out of my element and trying to survive being manipulated and often bullied, I would psyche myself up before entering the school building each day. I would imagine putting on the armor of God, taking a deep breath, creating a "survival" mind-set, and walking above whatever the trials of the day lay ahead. I put on a smile and opened the door . . . every day. I suppose that my past experiences as a full immersion, independent problem-solver helped me to excel, but those first years in public education were harrowing!

CHARLES SPURGEON STATED, "Nothing teaches us about the preciousness of the Creator as much as when we learn the emptiness of everything else."

Until I was blessed to have a few very special people come into my world, teaching was an emotionally barren wasteland for me. Each of those friendships allowed me to keep moving forward, if only for a brief time. Because of these people, I was able to focus on what I was learning, feel proud of the work I did, and enjoy the families I got to know and the children I helped to develop a positive self-image.

God demonstrated to me that sometimes the best we can do is simply be there. I tried to keep my focus on doing what I could with compassion, enthusiasm, and a sense of humor, building relationships as best I could, and trying not to be angered by the selfish games of others. Do I have regrets? Only for the anxiety I allowed myself to feel when I should have trusted God's leadership. The opportunities I was able to take advantage of were amazing. I became a much more effective teacher. I accepted the challenge of learning to create curriculum and assessments, and to work with district and state level educational leadership, which opened my eyes to a world I would never have had access to without making the decision to move into the public education arena. I met some wonderful people who are still in my life today, and I learned to recognize strengths in myself that I did not see before and certainly did not give myself credit for, not until saying "yes" to taking a chance.

No regrets? None, because no one need regret doing the best they can with what they know for all the right reasons. Can we control other people? No, we cannot. What we need to remember is that God knows, cares, and is in control. Our responsibility lies in asking for His guidance to remain steadfastly walking in His path each day. When we are faced with something that exceeds our own strength and ability, the Holy Spirit is our constant helper. God's wholeness, knowing that everything has a purpose and comes together for good, can and should be our peace. With this in our hearts, there is no "I can't"; rather, all things are possible. We must understand that the journey is just as important as the end result.

Consider asking yourself, "What will I miss if I don't try?" No "chickening out," as Uncle Johnny would say.

Just imagine the possibilities!

As the saying goes, "You are never too old to set another goal or to dream another dream."

I said, Days should speak, and multitude of years should teach wisdom. (Job 32:7)

TWENTY-NINE

LUNCH BOXES AND HOLIDAY GREETING CARDS

If you are an empathetic person, or simply easily touched by moments that draw you into a memory, you will understand how the changes in life trigger reminiscences of the past. Some of them can be amazingly wonderful, and some are exceedingly sad and draining.

Retirement afforded more discretionary time than I had had in years, so I focused on reconnecting. Be forewarned if you do this, there are surprises.

Perhaps it's because I'm so focused on connections—quick to wonder about the how and why I am at this place, feeling what I am and trying to gain perspective on the past—that so many things create twinges of recall and emotions.

For example, when the insulated canvas lunch tote I carried food in back and forth to school fell out of its storage place on the shelf of my kitchen pantry cupboard, my mind became flooded with memories. I recalled the goodies I carried in it, the way I felt when my hunger was satiated, how many times that canvas lunch tote was squashed into my school bag with my lesson plans and the eternal supply of papers to grade.

I thought about the students I shared food with (often little grape tomatoes and carrot sticks) because they came with so little fresh produce to eat. I remember being surprised that my food was always so intriguing to them, and that having a tomato or carrot from Mrs. Koenig's bag was such a treat. I remember spending some lunch hours tutoring students, and their concern that I find time to eat my lunch (the compassion that some children have is inspiring).

I thought about the field trips we took and how enthused my students were about where we were, what we were learning—and about getting to eat lunch with their teacher.

In other words, something as simple as a small black canvas lunch tote sent me on an amazing virtual journey.

I experienced another walk down memory lane the first Christmas season of my retirement as I dug out my box of Christmas cards, including those received over the years.

I remembered how important an annual tradition this was for my mother. It was an opportunity to touch the lives of friends and family in a more personal way than she had before. For her it was an essential ritual, done with Christmas music in the background, taking several days to complete.

I had not held on to the same tradition like she had. For years, holidays had provided a break from the usual daily routine of planning and running my classroom. The additional celebratory activities began to feel like just more things to do. My Christmas card list became abbreviated, and I made as many contacts as possible electronically. Often the cards I did send were late arriving at their destinations because I did not get to them until after the holiday break began.

My card box contained greetings from current friends, distant friends, and coworkers, as well as former students and their families. I reread all of them, laughing at the goofy photos and cherishing the timeless wishes of seasonal joy. I reread some with tears—in particular the last greetings from loved ones no longer physically here.

One such letter was from Aunt Betty and Uncle Bill telling me that Aunt Helen had passed away during the year. Aunt Betty had called me a few months later telling me that Uncle Bill was not doing well and had been moved into a nursing facility. She did not want me to hear this from anyone other than her. How precious that phone conversation was, for sadly, she died before Uncle Bill, so holiday letters stopped coming. What treasures these have become to me! These and our wedding photos are all the keepsakes I have of voices now silent.

Losing my brother, Denny's mom, and my career over the course of one year inspired me to search online for the contact information of folks far away that I needed to update on the events and losses in my life. If you ever find yourself searching online for loved ones you've lost touch with, prepare yourself, as obituaries pop up quickly. Reality struck hard as name after name brought up such a notice.

I found myself, hours later, needing to ask God for encouragement to close out this part of my thinking and move on. Fortunately, the last of the searches brought up the joyous knowledge that three people I feared gone were indeed very much alive at the advanced ages of eighty-four, eighty-seven, and ninety-seven. One was still preaching an occasional Sunday sermon at his church! An audio link to his most recent message was available—and what a blessing to hear his voice again! *Thank you, Lord, for providing answers to prayer. Thank you for memories generated from the simple things of life, like lunch boxes and holiday greeting cards. Thank you for reminders of what all these folks have meant to me and for helping me rejoice in where I am now. Time has a wonderful way of showing us what really matters. Help us not to waste it.*

So teach us to number our days, that we may apply our hearts unto wisdom. (Psalm 90:12)

THIRTY

NECESSARY ENDINGS

In her devotional *A Book of Prayer*, Stormie Omartian shares some of the astounding insights she gained from the challenges of her early life. Several of these prayers pertain to letting go of the past, embracing the future, and allowing God to guide us in using the talents He gave us. Her words have been such a blessing to me that I wanted to share them. I have chosen to include just brief excerpts that focus on the needs I have addressed in my life.

Lord, Lift Me Out of My Past

Set me free from my past, deliver me, heal me, help me let go of anything I have held onto of my past that has kept me from moving into all You have for me. Enable me to put off all former ways of thinking and feeling and remembering (Ephesians 4:22–24). Give me the mind of Christ so I will be able to understand when I am being controlled by memories of the past. I release my past to You and everyone associated with it so You can restore what has been lost.[1]

Lord, thank You that You make all things new and You are making me new each day (Revelation 21:5). Help me to keep my eyes looking straight ahead and to forgive what needs at be forgiven. I know You want to do something new in my life today. Help me to concentrate on where I am to go now and not where I have been. Release me from the past so I can move out of it and into the future You have for me. Do not remember the former things, nor consider the things of old. Behold, I will do a new thing . . . I will even make a road in the wilderness and rivers in the desert (Isaiah 43:18–19).[2]

Lord, Bless Me in the Work I Do

Thank You for the abilities You have given me. Where I am lacking in skill help me to grow and improve so that I do my work well. Open doors of opportunity to use my skills and close doors that I am not to go through. Give me wisdom and direction about that. I commit my work to You, Lord, knowing You will establish it (Proverbs 16:3). May it always be that I love the work I do and be able to do the work I love. Establish the work of my hands so that what I do will find favor with others and be a blessing for many. May it always be glorifying to You.[3]

I would add this: *God, help me to manifest the fruit of the Spirit: love, joy, peace, long-suffering, kindness, goodness, faithfulness, gentleness, self-control* (Galatians 5:22–23).

. . .

WHAT HAVE I learned from my journey thus far?

I learned that while I can't change my past, it doesn't determine my future. I am not destined to repeat anything if I am instead aware of it and change.

I learned that resolving past issues is done through the process of forgiveness. Looking honestly at problems, facing them, letting them go, and grieving losses frees us from the past so we can see people as they are. My father's parents had their struggles. That was not his fault. His older sister was institutionalized with mental illness until the time of her death at age forty-five. That was not his fault. He was called upon to serve in the navy during WWII and did so. He was a successful businessman for a number of years and, I believe, tried to be a dad to my brother for as long as he could prior to his mental decline. My father's mental illness was not his fault. Mental illness is incredibly devastating, certainly to the afflicted person but also to those who are left picking up the pieces under overwhelming uncertainty, sadness, and often anger. These things I understand, and so I try to reconcile his limitations with his behavior to grieve less what might have been different.

I learned that I love my mother and am thankful to her for all she did for me. She did the best she could with what she knew and the tools she had. I don't know much about her mother's nurturing skills, but I believe that my mom lacked parenting knowledge that might have helped her better prepare me for the challenges of my life. Had she been taught better strategies for handling strong emotions—expectations and disappointments, grief and loss—she might have had more to offer me as I struggled to overcome my own anxieties, insecurities, and gigantic learning curves.

What did I lack that I wish she could have provided?

- A safe, predictable, stable home environment.
- Basic trust of those closest to me—personal security.
- Validation and acceptance of myself—perfection not required.
- Self-confidence—I belong—I am worthy.
- Hope, optimism—no guilt for wanting choices. (NOT "Don't get your hopes up and you won't be disappointed.")
- Communication—emotions are okay. (NOT "Don't feel that way.")

What would I ask her to change if I could?

- Please don't expect me to be your everything— daughter, sister, best friend, confidante.
- Please don't suffocate me or make me feel guilty for wanting to be my own person.
- Please don't assume that I want to do or am able to do what you expect of me as a caregiver.

CHILDHOOD EXPERIENCES and trauma can make establishing boundaries difficult later in life. What is considered normal and acceptable? When is saying no okay? Personally, I felt stifled, broken, and invisible for so much of my life that these became "normal" for me. Only recently did I come to realize that many of my default responses were not best.

Trying harder wasn't working. Taking responsibility for people and things I had no control over wasn't working. It was necessary to embrace the question of "Who am I and where am I going now?"

I applied my full immersion strategies (focus, drive, resilience) to changing my "victim" mind-set. I began choosing to invite kind, accepting, nurturing people into my life, and to accept responsibility for only what is mine to shepherd. I began reaching for excellence instead of perfection and appreciating how far I have come in allowing God to create a new and best version of me.

WHAT IF THINGS had been different?

For my father: Would a strong mind have allowed him to be the kind of dad his children needed him to be, and husband his wife needed? Would he have chosen to be those things?

For my brother: Without his accident, would he have become a compassionate physician who empathized with the struggles his patients faced? Would he have had a powerful testimony, or would he have been someone I would not recognize instead?

For my mother: How much different might her life have been if she had a son and husband who were physically and mentally whole? How might her marriage have worked out differently? What might she have done with her life had she not had to support David's rehabilitation? Would she have been so dependent on me? Would she have had what she wanted . . . all of us together in Grand Rapids? Would she have lived longer or more fully prior to losing her battle with Alzheimer's?

For me: What would a normal childhood and adolescence have looked like for me? How might my adult life have been different without all the caregiving responsibilities? Would I have been full immersion, a high achiever in high school and college? Would I have felt safer, more confident? What might my relationship with David have been? Would we have lost sixteen years in distant silence before reconnecting? Would I have driven for two days rushing to say good-bye just hours before he passed? How would my story be different with Denny? Would I be on the path I'm on now?

Growing up is not for sissies! David and I were, whether separately or together (and definitely in our individual ways), searching for wholeness as we strived to fit the pieces of our fragmented, emotionally baggage-laden lives together to create "self." We were striving for a sense of control, ownership, and worthiness that was so difficult to maintain. Determined to create lives that were spiritually centered and emotionally fulfilling.

Yes, we'd grown up having somewhat different experiences, but we still had so much in common. Dad threw David away, and in losing himself to mental illness, he threw my mom and me away too. The collateral damage generated from this devastation created insurmountable challenges for all of us for a lifetime. Hard to escape! Hard to heal!

The deaths of my father, mother, and brother leave me the keeper of the memories, the storyteller, the remaining survivor, trying to find peace with the past and strength for the future. My purpose and my challenge is to be a blessing, to share with others (you) the struggles, the strategies, and the strength I have experienced in my life. I have found that we are stronger than we think we are so much of the time.

Remember, God is in every moment, guiding our days, until His will is accomplished for each of our lives. Of this I have no doubt. Do we need to fix everything, be perfect? We do not. Perfection is not required . . . only listening, trusting, and doing what matters, what we believe is our best today—the "live like you are dying," "good stuff" best. God takes care of the rest. He is already in tomorrow and beyond. Choose to accept that you are enough in God's eyes. What a blessing that truth is! The answers exist to all of our questions, and they will be revealed when we are ready to receive them. He knows how the story ends.

[God is] a father of the fatherless. (Psalm 68:5)

Be strong and of good courage. . . . for the Lord your God is with you wherever you go. (Joshua 1:9 NKJV)

And let the peace of God rule in your hearts, to the which also ye are called in one body; and be ye thankful. (Colossians 3:15)

EPILOGUE

I have always loved a well-crafted story—reading one, writing one, telling one. I became an entertaining tale teller (at least for nine- and ten-year-olds) in an attempt to capture my students' attention and captivate them long enough to teach my lesson objectives. They were often so engaged in my "dramedy" that they did not realize they were learning.

My topics included my cats, Ginger and Dixie, who were frequently the focus of conversation because of their crazy antics (like the time Dixie got stuck in the shower with the water running); my travels, experiences, and goofy observations (like "What do cows think about all day?"); and my imaginings about what it was like to be a historic character or pioneer in our national story (like "There was no Walmart on the corner for snacks along the Santa Fe trail").

I now feel a bit like the pioneers I loved to teach about—people with great drive and determination to make a better life for themselves and their families. Leaving the familiar, predictable behind (like my teaching career) and traversing large expanses of distance (like my past) to what was largely unknown and hugely challenging at best (like writing as my new chosen form of communication).

Pioneer commitment = full immersion, total intensity, focus, creative problem-solvers reaching the goal, the end of their journey. Much like my own.

Pioneer goal = reaching that new and better life. Much like my own.

Pioneer faith = investing themselves, letting go of the past, relying on God, family, and friends in the wagon train. These were smart, dedicated, hardworking, practical, humble, kind, generous, respectful, resilient people (for the most part) who demonstrated grit and a growth mind-set that believed "I can." Much like my own.

Fortunately, I have a teammate, my husband, Denny, who shares these pioneer-like traits: a combination of determination and perseverance, a willingness to continue on in the face of difficulties, being constantly driven to grow and improve. Age and experience cultivate maturity and wisdom, a different perspective than we had when we were much younger. God is with us always, but in hindsight, as we reflect on the miracles we've witnessed over time, in those moments He seemed to show up suddenly. I pray that you are aware of His presence in your life every day, but that you are also thrilled by His miraculous workings as you look back on your story.

My hope is that I have shared my life story in a valuable manner that blesses and supports you in your life. I am reasonably certain that

- you have had or are having struggles and are

working through them such that you can see yourself in some piece of my story.

- you understand the implications of full immersion because it describes you or someone you know.
- you believe that God loves us and leads us where He wants us to be, often by closing the doors He wants to close, and that He waits for us to be ready to move through the ones He opens. Sometimes it's painful and takes much longer than we wish.
- you are ready to embrace the possibilities of what's ahead in your life.

MY PRAYER IS that I have fulfilled my goals in sharing: providing a good story, full immersion style, providing connections for you to another person who has survived in spite of adversity, who has chosen to forgive and accept that all things have a purpose even though it may not seem evident in the moment. A person who inspires others to accept themselves and reach for excellence rather than perfection. A person who believes in choosing to do what makes one's heart sing. We are worthy . . . we matter!

NOTES

Chapter 11

1. Charles F. Stanley, *How to Handle Adversity* (Nashville: Thomas Nelson, 1989), 71.

Chapter 27

1. Fred Rogers, *The World According to Mr. Rogers: Important Things to Remember* (New York: Hachette Books, 2003), 389.
2. C. S. Lewis, *The Problem of Pain* (New York: HarperCollins, 2012; 1940), 91.

Chapter 30

1. Stormie Omartian, *A Book of Prayer: 365 Prayers for Victorious Living* (Eugene, OR: Harvest House, 2006), 82.
2. Stormie Omartian, *A Book of Prayer,* 83.
3. Stormie Omartian, *A Book of Prayer,* 33.

ABOUT THE AUTHOR

Nancy Koenig retired from education after spending thirty-nine years teaching grades K-12. She is well versed on the joys and challenges of caregiving, having spent many decades caring for her mother and quadriplegic brother.

In her writing, she uses her love of family and history to explore issues that matter to women of all ages.

Today Nancy is a newlywed of seventeen years, and lives with her husband, Denny, and two cats, Ginger and Dixie, in Colorado Springs, Colorado.

Connect with Nancy on Facebook at:
www.Facebook.com/AuthorNancyKoenig.